POWER AND PRECEDENT:
THE ROLE OF LAW IN THE UNITED STATES

POWER AND PRECEDENT:
THE ROLE OF LAW IN THE UNITED STATES

By

Jan G. Deutsch

VANDEPLAS PUBLISHING

UNITED STATES OF AMERICA

Power and Precedent:
The Role of Law in the United States

Deutsch, Jan G.

Published by:

Vandeplas Publishing
January 2007

801 International Parkway
5th Floor
Lake Mary, FL. 32746
USA

www.vandeplaspublishing.com

ISBN: 978-1-60042-014-6
Library of Congress Control Number: 2006940448
© 2007 Jan G. Deutsch

Printed in the United States of America

For Barbara

Table of Contents

		Page
Chapter 1	**Introduction: What This Course is About**	1
	My Years on the Supreme Court:	
	Becoming an American	1
	Law and the Election of 2004	8
	Cases and Precedents	15
Chapter 2	**The Judicial Process**	17
	Art, Law and the United States	17
	A. The Art of Law	17
	B. Law and the United States	29
	Judging, the Civil War and the Common Law	45
	A. Holmes, Law and the Civil War	45
	B. Judges, Philosophy and the Common Law	55
Chapter 3	**Power and Culture**	63
	Analyzing Capitalist Democracy	63
	Leadership and the Party	71
	Politics and Economics	77
Chapter 4	**Law, Politics and President Clinton**	81
	Law and the Art of Politics	81
	The Science of Politics	93
	Judging the Politics of Capitalist Democracy	96
Chapter 5	**The Platonic Form of United States Law**	103
	Judging and the Philosopher King	103
	Constitution of the State of Utopia	106
	A Philosophy of Law	109
Chapter 6	**A Post-Hegelian Jurisprudence: Holmes, Hand and Cardozo**	123
	Pennsylvania Coal Company v. Mahon	123
	The Mystery of Law	138

CHAPTER 1:
INTRODUCTION: WHAT THIS COURSE IS ABOUT

My Years on the Supreme Court:
Becoming an American

I

I am an American; but not by birth. Consequently, when I analyze that claim (doing what lawyers are trained to do) I arrive at what, for me, is an intriguing question: Exactly when did it happen? The answer (though I didn't understand it at the time) is the two years I spent clerking for Justice Potter Stewart.

II

At Yale College I learned my version of what it meant to be middle class, which is what I believed defined an American. Harvard was elitist, and, while Marxists said that being bourgeois was just a matter of socio-economic process, I was sure that there was more to the game of life than process, that even if winning (at least in college football) had something arbitrary about it, playing well meant defining oneself in a positive way.

I was too naïve to ask myself whether being American wasn't precisely the faith that winning proved that one had played the game well; and that naiveté was concretized for me during my student years at Yale Law School, the early years of the trajectory that enabled the Law School to win, to surpass its rival on the Charles. As I understood it, Yale was applying the advertising technique later associated with Avis: "We may not be No. 1, but we're different and therefore we're better." All my teachers seemed to me to agree that Harvard understood how to produce good lawyers, and that, while Harvard may have been too closely tied to the case method of teaching, the difference was not one of process, but of substance; Harvard had doubts about *Brown*, doubts not about the result, but technical questions about the propriety of relying on social science rather than overruling *Plessey v. Ferguson*, the case which had promulgated the separate-but-equal doctrine.

The problem presented by *Brown* is that it changed the law without being clear about how it had done so, leaving vague just what had replaced the prior rules. *Brown* made law by conscious reliance on the political device of the coded message, of meaning something that only the initiated would understand. Thus, if *Brown* were to be effective, it would require lawyers to become not only an elite, but a self-conscious elite, implementing a social change by attributing to the law a certainty it lacked. America being a capitalist country, this meant that lawyers were entitled to substantially greater monetary rewards than they had earned pre-*Brown*, before their elite status had been acknowledged.

At the time, I was aware only that the federalism that had been undermined politically by the New Deal's transfer of power to the central government was being undermined in the legal system by the need to enforce *Brown*, that the question whether the last word in a given matter belonged to the state or federal government was increasingly treated as a question answered by citing the 14th Amendment. The legal issue, of course, was usually which precedent was relevant rather than whether or not federalism was a more important value than the policy goal being argued for; and the lesson I learned as a clerk was the connection between precedent and judging, the technical concept and the political result.

III

Socrates was confrontational, not because he knew the answer, but because he knew that we learn effectively, if at all, from our failures; and both Yale and Harvard at least formally treated Socratic questioning as the basis for effective legal education. My failure was the attempt, in *School District v. Schempp*, to develop a theory that would avoid making the free exercise and establishment clauses contradictory. I believed that such a theory would provide the basis for the Justice's dissent in that school prayer case, from which he eventually dissented on technical grounds, that coercion had not been proved and that the state statute at issue could be read sufficiently flexibly to obviate any coercion.

My attempt was produced by dissatisfaction with his earlier dissent in *Engel v. Vitale*, in which he cited, *inter alia*, examples of religious practices in Congress and religious references in the Pledge of Allegiance, on coins, and in the National Anthem to justify his conclusion that the Regents' Prayer in the State of New York ("Almighty God, we acknowledge our dependence upon Thee, and we beg Thy blessings upon us, our parents, our teachers and our country") was not an "official religion," a constitutional "establishment".

I now understand that the *Engel* result made *Schempp* inevitable, that if one struck down an attempt consciously to encompass as many religious beliefs as possible, one was obviously holding that constitutional rights are absolute rather than situational, and so stand independent of the context in which they arise. In legal terms, this means that one cannot be equitable in applying such a right. Yet it was the hypothetical possibility of the equitable precedent that made me an American, someone who believed that the Rule of Law encompasses justifiable exceptions as well as absolute directives.

I felt that Stewart was someone I would want to be the judge if I were on trial for murder because, unlike the other Justices, he seemed to care, not about theory or doctrine, but only about the correct result in the particular case. My articulation was that Stewart decided cases as a judge rather than a Justice. But I overlooked the fact that he had only recently been elevated to the Supreme Court, that he had not yet joined sufficient opinions to begin to hear arguments structured, not on precedents, but on his own holdings. Sooner or later, in other words, the need to make rulings consistent forces a Supreme Court Justice to make doctrine as well as decide the particular case.

The question remains, however, what being an American means today, when a judge who believes in the equitable precedent, that rights are defined by context and are therefore situational rather than absolute, can be confirmed as a Justice only if the majority of the Senate defines itself as conservative.

IV

America is a capitalist country, in which the Rule of Law is accepted as the necessary constraint on a market that values the results of the game. The difficulty is that separation of powers was consciously designed to produce inefficiency, to impede the application of political power; and what the market values is efficiency. As a result, the only proposition on which all Justices agreed while I was clerking was that what they were doing was something other than politics; but that proposition could remain valid only so long as the President and the Congress continued to behave as though it was true.

The problem presented to the legal process by separation of powers is best analyzed by examining the claim, embodied in *Brown*, that the 14th Amendment should be read as applying against the states rights which the Founders intended to restrict only the central government. That Amendment, like a judicial opinion for the Court (or a clear majority thereof), is the result of a process as well as being the justification for a particular result. The process is that of achieving consensus, reaching agreement on means as well as ends, possible meanings as well as likely results.

One ascertains the meaning of a legislative enactment, in other words, by treating it as a precedent, finding the denominator common to the largest number of possible interpretations, the issue on which unity was most likely achieved. In the case of the 14th Amendment, that was the overruling of *Dred Scott*, the Supreme Court decision that had read the Constitution as defining slaves as property rather than persons. Separation of powers, however, makes such a narrow reading impermissible, since in theory the branches are equal as well as independent, which means that laws control the future but cannot invalidate a prior judicial act.

This theory, moreover, is the basis for the power exercised by each of the branches, as well as a restriction upon exercise of that power. *Marbury v. Madison*, for example, effectively established the right of the Court to hold acts of the legislature unconstitutional because the Congress was rendered helpless by a Court decision that refused to accept an authority to act granted to it by the Congress. Similarly, that the Executive can base its acts on an interpretation of the Constitution inconsistent with an Act of Congress or Supreme Court decision is a statement of historical fact as well as constitutional theory. The issue our country faces today, therefore, is that of defining itself in realistic terms, either granting supremacy to one branch or re-defining what we mean by the Rule of Law, or forcing each appellate judge to write an individual opinion detailing how her or his result was reached.

So long as we refuse to replace common (or constitutional) law rights with bureaucratic civil law directives, or make common law transparent by requiring individual opinions, demanding a particular view of precedent is questioning good faith, a judge's fidelity to the Rule of Law. The Supreme Court makes the law much as a lobbyist makes the law, by making clear to the legislature what is entailed by a particular application of a legislative directive; and when precedents are lacking, or conflicting, or subject to interpretation, how a judge decides is ultimately the question how she or he feels about the facts presented by the case.

Being an American today thus involves coming to terms with the fact that belief that a system of separation of powers will produce the right result requires an act of faith. The basis for that faith was analyzed by two immigrants, who developed contrasting theological definitions of Protestantism for the society that produced *Brown*. Reinhold Niebuhr, like *Brown,* accepted social science as defining the context for action, but he insisted that that context would teach humans that their sinful nature required the goodness of the Almighty. Paul Tillich made the issue substantive, by defining the Divine as a mystery, incomprehensible to the human mind. One does not necessarily have to agree with Tillich to apply to politics the insight that the meaning of an operational faith may be mysterious even to the person whose faith it is. Unless one does, however, there seems no alternative to the conclusion that winning five votes is the only way humans have of determining whether the Supreme Court has reached the right result.

Law and the Election of 2004

It is generally agreed that one of the best things John Kerry did was to concede without resorting to law to challenge the election result. The question raised by this fact is how United States law has become, in this instance, something feared by the public it purportedly serves.

I

The first step is to be precise about the fact which this essay purports to explain. Because the challenge would not change the outcome, the use of law to challenge the result would be justified by appeal to a higher law: morality or constitutional principle. Claims such as this were often made in connection with resistance to the Vietnam War, and recent years have seen a variety of governmental enactments and activities which, while accepted as legal, can be seen as incompatible with the Bill of Rights. RICO and the Patriot Act are examples. They differ in that RICO can be seen as an attempt to deal with a purely domestic issue, but it is the argument of this essay that the 2004 election result was a response to cultural changes, and that central to those changes was a perception of law as a tool used to bring about social change.

To say that the political center has moved rightward is to confuse a characterization with an explanation. American political parties have always competed to win elections rather than to impose their ideological prescriptions on the society they were competing to rule. Consequently, the contest has always been to attract those not yet committed to either party.

What has happened is that neither party is willing to treat the avowed position of the other as advanced in good faith. Thus, neither party officially supported gay marriage, since both understood that a majority of Americans disapproved of discrimination against gays but treated any attempt to change the legal (as opposed to social) concept of marriage as a step too far. Yet gay marriage was clearly an issue. Similarly, the question of the right to life was sidestepped by proponents of partial birth abortion despite the fact that the facts of such abortions raise precisely that issue.

The 2004 election, in short, was about bringing to consciousness that, in the United States, law – because it does not resolve disputes so much as simply delaying their resolution until the emotions involved have had opportunities to be diverted to new issues – has historically been used to defuse issues too "hot" for the political processes. *Brown v. Board of Education* enlisted the judiciary in the effort to resolve "hot" issues, and the 2004 election result is an attempt to call a halt to use of the law consciously to implement social change, perception of the law as a means rather than an end.

II

When I was a law student, my education began by being told that law was different from higher education, a matter of learning rather than being taught; that Socratic questioning rather than lectures was the way we would learn the law: and that the goal of that questioning was skeptical humility, skeptical because everything was open to question, and humility because the Socratic process made one aware that the teacher was not alone in her or his uncertainty, that, in the end, neither logic nor feeling was an unerring guide to what the law ought to be.

It was this knowledge about the difficulty of moving from the instance to the rule that gave one respect for the concept of precedent, that forced one to recognize that law was a matter of art rather than science, of persuasive analogy rather than statistical proof; and it is this knowledge which has been discarded as law has increasingly become a justification for change rather than a search for the right result.

Precedent does not mean, of course, that the law ignores the need for change, that the equity of a particular set of facts justifies the judge in using the law to impede necessary progress. The question always is how far is too far or what shade of gray is appropriate. Law, if it is effective, is social as well as individual, political as well as legal truth; and litigators are therefore best seen as free knights, actors on the legal stage whose roles (and justifications) involve the concrete applications of theory necessary for the resolution of disputes. The question raised by 2004 is where the line between the legal and the political should be drawn, what the limits on the litigators' arguments should be, and whether such limits on theoretical possibilities can be enforced.

III

Brown was a decision dealing with state educational systems, and the attempt to implement it in the face of resistance on the part of state and some lower federal judges meant that the Supreme Court increasingly curtailed the area of law subject to exclusive state control. The Supreme Court is now trying to reverse that process, to grant more power to state governments, but *Bush v. Gore* demonstrates that federalism no longer functions as the cultural given that makes the United States different, a social entity in which loyalty is owed to two competing politically sovereign authorities. Thus, Justice O'Connor signaled at the oral argument what the result in *Bush v. Gore* would be when she stressed that the elections at issue were federal in nature, a fact which suggested that state court interference (at least once the Supreme Court had acted by refusing to intervene, even if it had not explained its inaction in a written opinion) was illegitimate. Only so long as federalism was accepted as a given, however, could O'Connor's clear line be drawn, and a Court self-conscious about the power it was exercising therefore felt it necessary to justify its result with theories such as that in the Scalia opinion.

The law *Marbury v. Madison* expounded, something that existed apart from the opinions of individual Justices, is another of the historical givens that have become cultural anachronisms. Law, in short, is no longer a reality one accepts but a goal oriented political process, protective of the rights to which one is entitled. In addition to federalism, the individual in the United States is protected by the system of separation of powers, and the equality of those three branches implies a liberty for each, because each branch is enabled to treat the law as a tool rather than an end on the basis that the other two branches can be relied on to check excesses. This is a liberty which is not available to courts where no written Constitution exists, and it is that liberty which underlies what happened in *Brown*.

Brown was justified because segregation was a problem which neither the legislature nor the executive was going to solve. The judiciary, however, had itself added to the problem by the decisions in *Dred Scott* and *Plessy v. Ferguson* and, rather than explicitly overruling the latter, or reading the Fourteenth Amendment as overruling the former (rather than as transforming a Bill of Rights directed against the federal government into a tool used to limit state sovereignty), the *Brown* court attempted to justify its results by relying on social science. The problem we face today is a reluctance to accept cultural change justified by such decisions, by courts taking advantage of the liberty granted them by the Constitution rather than following precedent.

IV

The law I learned was a system that defined questions rather than providing answers, and while I cannot argue that we can afford such a system, this course hopes to persuade you that its replacement is inadequate to the tasks being assigned to it. Thus, the culture we live in today is one that stresses rights, a democratization, so to speak, of the court of Louis XIV. We may not be aristocrats, in other words, but the people in power need our votes, and their goal should therefore be to provide our happiness rather than to set our goals. I propose this analogy because it was de Tocqueville who most clearly described both the possibilities and perils of our system and when, in *Ancien Regime*, he analyzed his own society, he assigned to the aristocrats in Louis XIV's court responsibility for the weakening of checks on political authority that resulted in the French Revolution.

The Founders of our nation were implementing the ideals of the Enlightenment (albeit in its Scottish rather than the French variation) but our nation came into existence before the French Revolution occurred. It is only since World War II that we have been forced to face the possibility that revolutions are domestic versions of the need for change embodied in a declaration of war, that rights represent the willingness to run the risks of anarchy, and that RICO and the Patriot Act represent responses to those possibilities, the sorts of possibilities that were realized in the French Revolution.

How one responds to this situation is a philosophical as well as cultural question, because science is itself a process about which one can be skeptical. Social science is not historical truth because events are overdetermined. What happens cannot be analyzed by holding all other things equal except in imagination. Accurate description, in other words, is in the end what we can hope to achieve, and that only if we do not accept convincing historical distortions as true.

Humans, in short, are the animals whose lives are defined by the impossible attempt to escape the uncertainty created by each other's existence. Consequently, my premise in this course is that students aspiring to be lawyers must learn to understand the past embodied in precedents rather than how to take the political risks involved in taking a position, in a student paper or judicial opinion. This course will attempt (insofar as we conclude it is possible) to deal with issues in the philosophy of law: What is law? Why does one obey law? How does one reach the right result? Even if those questions are not answerable, analysis of why they cannot be answered provides the basis for making a paper a learning experience. Whether judicial opinions achieve that status for the judge is a question in the philosophy of law.

Cases and Precedents

What distinguishes a case from a precedent? The technical answer is citation of the opinion by judges in future cases, but that technicality *is* the common law, and this course is an attempt to define that phenomenon.

Defining the phenomenon is what Socrates was attempting to do when he created the concept Plato popularized as the Form, and the Socratic quest for a definition of the Rule of Law requires an exploration of the history that created that concept, the human ideas and historical forces that produced Great Britain and the United States, countries ruled by common rather than civil law.

The quest is made difficult by the fact that human behavior is not only psychological or sociological or political or economic, but all of the above. Economics is a "hard" science because it is materialistic, dealing with goods and services and how they are produced and distributed. Psychology and sociology deal with processes that motivate human behavior in terms of the person and the group. Culture and character are embodied in such behavior. And our personal behavior is significantly affected by our guess about how long we have to live, because being aware of the uncertainty of longevity underlies self-awareness, a person's response to the question "Where am I going?"

Science and art attempt to give us answers to that question by creating rational theory and emotional belief – the scientific formula, the personal symbol and social ideology – things that are used to justify action, behavior characterized as rational and/or emotional. All's fair in love and war, meaning that there are no formulas, no binding rules, but law involves judgment of behavior, and this course explores the connection between client behavior and the process of the law. The choice for the judge is that of change or the status quo, following the precedents or attempting to make new law, and human change can be characterized as spiritual – a change in character – as well as material, a change in behavior.

Spiritual changes are miracles, events humans may desire, but which they do not control. Changes in the material world cause or are caused by the politics of theory, changes in the concepts which structure our perception of the environment. Precedent is a powerful concept because it postulates that changes can be rational, balancing the constraints of theory, of the past, against the needs of the present and the theoretical possibilities of the future.

A lawyer, an officer of the court, is charged with counseling clients how to comply with human laws. The course materials analyze common law processes of adjudication that create legal opinions, some of which serve as precedents. The goal of the jurisprudence presented in the materials is to understand the connections between client behavior and those processes. The philosophy embodied in that jurisprudence is an attempt to set out those connections, to explore the meaning of the concept of precedent.

CHAPTER 2:
THE JUDICIAL PROCESS

ART, LAW, AND THE UNITED STATES
A. The Art of Law

I

This course defines law as applied politics and politics as the attempt to make cultural decisions conscious. Law is a cultural phenomenon and culture a social phenomenon, a set of aspirations defined by social value choices, a hierarchy of concepts imposed on individual behavior in the form of things done "because they have to be done that way," done that way even if the standard seems unduly harsh when applied to oneself. Culture, in other words, defines the human or group of humans who produce it, and, by so doing, can be treated as subscribing to the propositions to which culture is reduced by those attempting to comprehend other people's cultures.

Cultural choices are not biological and yet are made unconsciously or habitually, thus providing the basis for understanding decisions which are attributed to emotional forces or guesses about the future. Culture, in short, is what the individual experiences as socialization, the processes by means of which one identifies oneself as a member of a group. Humans, however, also engage in political events called revolutions which are perceived as attempts to change existing social value choices. From a political perspective, therefore, culture constitutes the precipitate of history, but history encompasses art and economics as well as society and politics.

Economics accounts for human behavior by postulating a rational pattern of human activity based on attempts to seek pleasure and avoid pain. The market is the theoretical construct in terms of which those attempts interact, and the applicability of the theory to any particular instance is necessarily limited by two factors: the extent to which the medium of exchange – money – has the same value for all participants and the existence of desires that cannot accurately be calculated in terms of pleasure and pain.

Capitalist societies tend to ignore these limitations, to prefer the structure of the economic market to that of the political law. Social reality, however, is accurately described in terms of rational economic calculation only to the extent that a society agrees on a coherent set of goals. Given overriding goals, even the cost of persuading people to pursue them can accurately be calculated. When the goals are not overriding, however, when the demand that creates the market is restricted to the desires of individual consumers, then the social calculus proves incapable of doing more than displaying the relative weights to be assigned to the particular amalgams of values in terms of which the relevant individuals define themselves.

The closest humans have come to establishing a system capable of comparing rather than displaying individual values is money; and it is money's symbolic role as the measuring rod of value that permits a blurring of the line between persuasion and coercion, that provides a counterweight to the values implicit in the complex of myths and institutions that constitute national character, the forces which effectively restrict behavior within socially approved boundaries. It nevertheless remains true that the value of a unit of money is determined by the emotional time frame of the particular person valuing that unit, a perspective that dictates how that person feels, whether what is important is tomorrow, next year, or eternity.

Art is the creation (sometimes only by implication) of patterns responsive to emotional demands rather than rational calculations, to the mysteries of transcendent goals and values as opposed to the delineation of measurable costs and benefits. The world is full of mysteries – how patterns emerge from an ongoing process that produces instances; how we create persons from ever-changing sets of personal feelings and social roles; how rules are adaptable to ever-changing circumstances – and these mysteries are embodied in the styles that characterize works of art which portray reality for us. The political choice of style is that of one's attitude towards the social truth embodied in the *status quo*, the currently accepted style, whether one sees one's task as creating variations or finding a better style. The choice described is that between a classical and romantic perspective, whether one sees oneself as a member of the group whose truth that style expresses, or as a revolutionary with values in terms of which the validity of that style can be assessed.

The connection between style and legal precedent, the meaning of an opinion and the way it is written, can be illustrated by examining *Palsgraf v. Long Island R.R.*, a case given to first-year law students to illustrate fundamental principles of law, and *Salmon v. Meinhard*, a precedent frequently quoted in defining the standard of conduct expected of corporate fiduciaries.

In August 1924, a cleaning lady from Brooklyn is standing on a railway platform in close proximity to some mail scales. At the other end of the platform, a man running to catch an already departing train is being pushed onto that train by two trainmen. This man is carrying a brown paper parcel which, unknown to the trainmen, contains firecrackers. The parcel falls, the firecrackers explode on impact, the shock dislodges the scales, the scales strike the cleaning lady, and she develops a stutter.

In 1902, Walter J. Salmon leases the Hotel Bristol for a twenty year term and finances improvements by entering into an agreement with Meinhard whereby he manages the venture while Meinhard supplies the capital. The profits are to be divided sixty/forty for five years and then shared equally, and all losses are to be shared equally. The venture succeeds, and in 1921 – four months before the expiration of the lease – Salmon is approached with a development scheme that includes the Hotel site. Without telling Meinhard, he establishes a realty company, which obtains a new lease.

Palsgraf begins: "Plaintiff was standing on a platform of defendant's railroad after buying a ticket to go to Rockaway Beach." And Meinhard: "On April 10, 1902, Louisa M. Gerry leased to defendant Walter J. Salmon the premises known as the Hotel Bristol...." Not once in *Palsgraf* does the judge write "Helen Palsgraf" or "Palsgraf"; always it is "plaintiff" or "she," whereas in *Meinhard* the parties are called by name.

Both opinions are written by the same judge, Benjamin Cardozo, who is attempting properly to define a legal duty and to answer the question whether that duty has been breached. In *Palsgraf* the answer is negative and in *Meinhard* the answer is positive. The reason for the divergence in results is apparent in the passage quoted from *Meinhard* as establishing the standard of conduct for corporate fiduciaries:

> Many forms of conduct permissible in a workaday world for those acting at arm's length are forbidden to those bound by fiduciary ties. A trustee is held to something stricter than the morals of the marketplace.... Only thus has the level of conduct for fiduciaries been kept at a level higher than that trodden by the crowd. It will not be consciously lowered by any judgement of this court.

Palsgraf was a transaction of the workaday world. There, the "morals of the marketplace", of the "crowd," rule; and the crowd, of course, is faceless. *Meinhard* was something else, something governed by stricter rules. Two men became bound to one another in a relationship that obliged them to a "level of conduct" "higher than that trodden by the crowd."

The *rationale* for *Meinhard* is clear. In *Meinhard*, Cardozo is concerning himself with the definition of justice in the circumstances before him rather than being governed by the past, focusing on the doing of equity rather than simply following the prior law. The difficulty is apparent:

> Equity is a roguish thing. For law we have a measure, know what to trust to: Equity is according to the conscience of him that is Chancellor, and as that is larger or narrower, so is Equity. 'Tis all one as if they should make the standard for the measure we call a "foot" a Chancellor's foot: what an uncertain measure would this be! One Chancellor has a long foot another a

short foot, a third an indifferent foot. 'Tis the same thing in the Chancellor's conscience.

In *Palsgraf*, moreover, it is Cardozo who is helping to make of law an efficient tool, establishing as clear a rule as possible and following it. The question, therefore, is the proper balance between following the law and doing equity, the relationship between justice and the law.

II

The judge whose work was marked by loyalty to the mechanism of precedent is Learned Hand, whose opinions painstakingly analyzed the facts in the case before him to demonstrate that the precedents, if properly understood, permitted but one result. Hand's loyalty to precedent was an attempt to deal with something he portrayed with perfect clarity in a commencement address he delivered in 1927:

> I speak but as I know, and yet I know beyond what I speak. For all of us are alike human creatures, and whether it be in building a house, or in planning a dinner, or in drawing a will, or in establishing a business, or in excavating an ancient city, or in rearing a family, or in writing a play, or in observing an epidemic, or in splitting up an atom, or in learning the nature of space, or even in divining the structure of this giddy universe, in all chosen jobs the craftsman must be at work, and the craftsman, as Stevenson says, gets his hire as he goes. Even this obdurate and recalcitrant world is perhaps in the end no more than a complicated series of formulae which we impose upon the flux. If so, we are throughout its builders, unconscious but always at work. In part at any rate, we consciously compose; and as we do, a happy fortuity gives us the sense of our own actuality, an escape from the effort to escape, a

contentment that the mere stream of consciousness cannot bring, a direction, a solace, a power and philosophy.

Precedent may, of course, be nothing more than "a complicated series of formulae which we impose upon the flux," but being bound by its rules offered Hand a philosophy, a structure in terms of which existence could be ordered and the power he exercised therefore legitimated. Thus, were we still ruled by a monarch, the question confronting the judge would simply be whether, in the circumstances presented, the monarch would make law or do justice, focus on the system of precedents or the circumstances of the particular case. Justice in a constitutional monarchy thus becomes identified with the judiciary as opposed to the legislature, with those who use the common law to adapt the legislature's general rule to the particular circumstances.

Hand, however, is making law in a democracy, as a member of an independent but still no more than co-equal branch of a divided government. Technically, the United States of America constitutes a republic rather than a democracy, and, in *The Republic*, Plato argues that a king, like Hand's judge applying precedent, must in so doing become a philosopher, devoting himself to ascertaining the proper action, the Form that is desired by those for whom law is being made. Because Plato's republic involves more than one participant, however, the question arises whether the phenomenon Plato is describing can withstand rational analysis.

Analysis implies a model defined in terms of cause and effect, and once more than a single human is involved, the acts produced by the model are by definition over-determined, in the sense that no single model can effectively account for all potential outcomes, for the consequences of humans responding to each other's behaviors. Plato solved this dilemma by presenting his propositions in the form of a dialogue rather than a model, and by producing a work, *The Republic*, which functions as a metaphor for both the citizen and community. The metaphor is made applicable by the fact that both citizen and community are known solely in terms of their actions, the manifestations of their beings, known as Forms.

The concept of Forms implies that reality is functional, that things are what they do, a formulation which involved Plato in a number of difficulties, not the least of which was an ambivalence towards art, whose "beings" – works of art that portrayed reality – threatened to undermine any attempt to impose a coherent framework on existence. Forms assume a society paradigmatically classical in nature, in which all participants are bound together in the search for the same objective truth, a society possible only if emotions – our word for the distortions feelings impose on the objective truth contained in Forms – are effectively projected into a pantheon of gods, a pattern of potentially conflicting urges as opposed to a single Entity.

The society in which Socrates (and Plato) lived accomplished this feat because the categories with which Greeks functioned were concrete, what individuals were and did, as opposed to abstract, a human reality "in here" co-existing with a Divine or scientific reality "out there" and hence more real than what humans perceive. In attempting to apprehend the Forms that for Socrates constituted reality, in other words, Greeks did not distinguish art from science, the concrete object from the theoretical abstraction, because in their world facts could not clearly be separated from values, because the questions "what exists?" and "why?" were for them a matter, not of knowledge but of action, not of authority but of investigation, a Socratic quest for proper behavior, a situation in which human action defines its own context.

Greeks believed that paradoxes were soluble, that responses had to be made to the Socratic inquiry, because they treated life as a matter of pattern rather than chaos, because, in short, they believed in law. Law became more concrete – and therefore separate from – the pattern of life when the pantheon of gods became an Entity, when emotions coalesced into an Entity known as the individual, analysis of which is problematic precisely in the ways *The Republic's* analysis of the reality of social obligation (the duties of citizenship) was problematic.

The difficulty raised by granting to the individual the status of an Entity independent of, and more complex than, the social roles assigned to him or her by the community is the question of the legitimacy of that assignment, of community power, the possibility of the romantic proposition that the only valid law is the one the individual recognizes as binding, that we should seek justice rather than accept the *status quo*. Socrates' questions in effect present that possibility, because the emotions they produce in us change so quickly and for such a variety of reasons that they constitute truths too complex to be contained within the objectively knowable structure of existence embodied in forms. Socrates' fate, therefore, precisely because he executed the judgement of the court, makes plausible the argument underlying Hand's loyalty to precedent: that what society seeks from the processes of law is stability, and that equity – the search for Socratic justice – is a matter of maxims enunciated by Polonius, Utopian formulae potentially in conflict with the law.

III

Hand's treatment of precedent, his sensitivity to the context given to a set of facts by a legal concept, was no doubt the product of his many years of service as a trial judge. Litigators tell competing stories, through the mouths of witnesses who in many instances have been made aware of the legal consequences of a given recollection. A good judge knows, in other words, that litigators are presenting the facts sufficiently to engage the feelings of the judge or jury so that contradictory possibilities – other ways of looking at those facts – are ignored. The style which characterizes the opinions of Oliver Wendell Holmes, Jr., like the loyalty to precedent which characterizes those written by Hand, represents a response to this situation.

" [Brandeis]", Holmes said, "always desires to know all that can be known about a case, whereas I am afraid that I wish to know as little as I can safely go on." "I long have said there is no such thing as a hard case. I am frightened weekly but always when you walk up to the lion and lay hold the hide comes off and the same old donkey of a question of law is underneath".

A reading of Holmes' opinions reveals that what he refers to as "question[s] of law" are resolved, not by adherence to precedent, but by the creation of it, not by seeking the applicable rule, but by fashioning the appropriate one. A famous Holmes opinion proposing a free speech test, for example, persuaded, not by examining the law, but by sketching the striking vignette, by setting out the hypothetical of the false cry of "fire" in a theater.

In his work as a judge, Oliver Wendell Holmes, Jr. both created precedent and made the dissent acceptable, leaving Americans with the possibility that it might be the opinion of the individual judge, rather than that of the Court, which contained the more accurate picture of what the law should be, that American law has both classical and romantic aspects. Thus, for Holmes, respect for precedent means that one treats the law as providing the context for action as opposed to defining the limits on one's activity.

Unlike Hand, therefore, Holmes writes opinions which are accurately described as works of art, and their success must be assessed, not on the basis of the significance of loyalty to precedent, but rather in terms of the validity of a given style. To ask whether a style is valid is to ask whether it conveys what the creator desires it to transmit. In such an investigation of motive, the personal testimony will be phrased in terms of process, that a given expression "fit" or that a particular phrase "felt right." If the issue is addressed in a social rather than personal context, the judgement concerning validity can be made either in economic or political terms. Economically, the process described by the creator works if it sells, if the market accepts or approves it. And politically, a style works if we buy it, if we see something we had been unaware of, if something we had known is made to "fit" as we feel it should, or if we feel that what is being said or written is authentic, is telling us how the author "really" feels. It is in this latter sense, the context of being offered something that in personal terms is normally reserved for the confessional, that law-making can be designated as artistic or spiritual in nature.

Holmes' approach to the making of law thus works as all good stories work, not by retailing the murky and confusing truth of how things are, but by appealing to emotions, by confirming our felt certainties about how we know they should be. As successful stories, Holmes' opinions explain the past sufficiently persuasively to be applicable to, and thus to influence, the future. A successful judge, in short, either follows precedent or makes a symbol of the legal sign known as precedent, thus transforming the artistic ambiguity of a word, a phrase or a description into a goal or a caution, a direction for future action or non-action.

The question that remains is the role this analysis of American law assigns to the attorney, how the power to tell the client what the law is should be exercised.

B. Law and the United States

Foreword

Visiting Americans and studying their laws, one discovers that the prestige accorded to lawyers and their permitted influence in the government are now the strongest barriers against the faults of democracy. I think this result can be traced back to a general cause worth examining, because it might recur elsewhere.

For five hundred years lawyers have taken part in all the movements of political society in Europe. Sometimes they have been the tools of the political authorities, and sometimes they have made those authorities their tools. In the Middle Ages the lawyers' cooperation was invaluable in extending the domination of the kings; they have since striven hard to restrict that same power. In England they have become closely united with the aristocracy; in France they have proved its most dangerous enemies. Do lawyers, then, yield to sudden and temporary impulses, or are they more or less obedient, according to circumstances, to constantly recurring instincts natural to them? I should like to get this matter clear, for it may be that lawyers are called on to play the leading part in the political society which is striving to be born.

Men who have made a special study of the laws and have derived therefrom habits of order, something of a taste for formalities, and an instinctive love for a regular concatenation of ideas are naturally strongly opposed to the revolutionary spirit and to the ill-considered passions of democracy.

Study and specialized knowledge of the law give a man a rank apart in society and make of lawyers a somewhat privileged intellectual class. The exercise of their profession daily reminds them of this superiority; they are the masters of a necessary and not widely understood science; they serve as arbiters between the citizens; and the habit of directing the blind passions of the litigants toward the objective gives them a certain scorn for the judgment of the crowd. Add that they naturally form *a body*. It is not that they have come to an understanding among themselves and direct their combined energies toward one objective, but common studies and like methods link their intellects, as common interest may link their desires.

So, hidden at the bottom of a lawyer's soul one finds some of the tastes and habits of an aristocracy. They share its instinctive preference for order and its natural love of formalities; like it, they conceive a great distaste for the behavior of the multitude and secretly scorn the government of the people.

deTocqueville, Democracy in America

I

The society created by the United States Constitution waited until 1865 before it resolved the concrete question of obedience raised by that Constitution. Prior to the Civil War, the United States functioned as a truly federal system, in that it was unclear whether primary loyalty was owed to the state or federal government. Law, therefore, and especially national law, could be viewed as an exceptional phenomenon, not intended to intrude on everyday activities. It was easy to accept federal law as necessarily supreme, in other words, so long as the community in which one's life was lived had rules of its own.

This state of affairs was made possible by the fact that courts in the United States were common-law courts, a judiciary whose law was the by-product of the work of resolving disputes. As a result, the obedience demanded was restricted to the precise decision rendered in the dispute being adjudicated. So long as one believed that a resolution, whatever its fairness, was preferable to an ongoing dispute, one could find judicial authority legitimate.

Until the Civil War, the Supreme Court had interpreted the commerce clause – the constitutional provision giving the federal Congress authority over commerce among the states – as permitting challenges to state laws designed to govern economic as opposed to social matters. Following that conflict, the clause was read more broadly, as mandating the establishment of a national market, and thus as overriding any state and local regulations, whatever their motivations, that had the effect of restricting commercial activities. Prior to the New Deal, however, the Court had not made clear the extent to which the model or ideology of the market was sufficient to override competing considerations in commerce clause cases. The New Deal was therefore revolutionary in the Court's acceptance of the power of Congress as the force responsible for regulating the economy.

The New Deal, in other words, was characterized by acceptance of a new truth about government and the law. When Roosevelt said that we "have nothing to fear but fear itself," he was reassuring the society he governed that the law could be replaced by a more effective force, that the economy could effectively be regulated by those who possessed the requisite knowledge. To some extent, Roosevelt was simply reverting to monarchical rhetoric, reassuring the population he ruled that he could be trusted. The promise was more than rhetoric, however, for Roosevelt implemented a structural revolution, legitimating direction of the economy by regulatory authorities. In functional terms, the expert replaced the law, and the application of technical expertise became accepted as something that advanced the public good.

A clear goal reduces the theoretical distinction between means and ends, instrumental and substantive acts, to a matter of technical expertise. Franklin Roosevelt's goal was clear, to "cure" the Depression, to make the market "recover." Operationally, the medical model proved to be an inappropriate metaphor.

The paradigmatic market is that of buying and selling stock, and one theory attributes the onset of the Depression to collapse of that market. That market, however, is driven by emotion – by greed for more and fear of loss – and the connection between that market and the operating economy is problematic at best, existing with certainty only in the tax lawyer's inability – at the margin – to distinguish (other than that they pay different rates of tax) between capital gains and income.

Thus, when things are going as they always have – which is what the models used by economists incorporate – sectors of the economy are of course inter-connected, but at any given moment, any given connection in the model may or may not be in operation. In general, further, (rather than at the margin), the decision whether to save (invest) or spend (consume) is determined by psychological rather than economic forces, by how one feels rather than the interest rate set by the central banking authorities. The consequence (and proof) of these propositions is that, when the United States entered World War II, it remained unclear whether or not "recovery" had taken place.

As a result, implementation of New Deal policies involved considerable strains, despite the fact that it was directed by one whom all acknowledge as a pre-eminent political practitioner. Dean Acheson recollects dealing with Roosevelt as his Under Secretary of the Treasury:

> "Then, too, came summonses to appear and report at the President's bedside while he breakfasted. Early bedside appointments started business for the President before the considerable period needed for him to be up and dressed. But they were not always as well adapted to the purpose as planned. After the tray was taken away, his daughter Anna's children – known as Sistie and Buzzie – often made a distracting entrance. Buzzie galloped about the room, while Sistie delighted in climbing onto the bed and sitting beside him. Then began a game not designed to improve communication between President and caller. The child, leaning innocently against her grandfather, would suddenly clap her hand over his mouth in the middle of a sentence, smothering the rest of it. The President's counterattack, a vigorous tickling of her ribs, brought her hand down in defense and produced joint hilarity. Conversation became intermittent, disjointed, and obscure."
>
> "Gay and informal as these meetings were, they nevertheless carried something of the relationship implied in a seventeenth century levée at Versailles. We think of these as stiff and formal, yet Saint-Simon tells us how Madam de Bourgoyne won a bet that she could sit on a chamber pot in the presence of the Sun King himself. This she did with the aid of her lady-in-waiting and her own voluminous skirts. Louis XIV could and did forgive her, his daughter-in-law. But, while the

relations between royalty and all the rest of humanity, however exalted, could be informal, they crossed a gulf measured by light years."

"The impression given me by President Roosevelt carried much of this attitude of European – not British – royalty. The latter is comfortably respectable, dignified, and bourgeois. The President could relax over his poker parties and enjoy Tom Corcoran's accordion, he could and did call everyone from his valet to the Secretary of State by his first name and often made up Damon Runyon nicknames for them, too –"Tommy, the Cork," "Henry, the Morgue," and similar names; he could charm an individual or a nation. But he condescended. Many reveled in apparent admission to an inner circle. I did not; and General Marshall did not, the General for more worthy reasons than I. He objected as he said, because it gave a false impression of his intimacy with the President. To me it was patronizing and humiliating. To accord the President the greatest deference and respect should be a gratification to any citizen. It is not gratifying to receive the easy greeting which milord might give a promising stable boy and pull one's forelock in return."

The New Deal was presented by Roosevelt as use of the power of the central government to combat the dangers of monopoly and corruption presented by those whose activities dominated interstate commerce, and a great deal of popular support was gained for the New Deal by this presentation; but when the Supreme Court impeded the implementation of a shift of power to the central government, Congress refused to assist the President in making the Court more responsive to that popular will. Defeat of Roosevelt's court-packing scheme did not mean, however, that the Court did not respond. Thus, for many years, the commerce clause was interpreted so liberally that it came to mean that Congress could assert national jurisdiction over a social or economic problem simply by identifying it.

In functional terms, moreover, the Court shifted its focus from that of maintaining the balance between state and federal authorities to that of protecting the citizen against the state and federal governments, thus transmuting the issue of the proper role of the Court in government into the question of the meaning of the Bill of Rights. Given this transmutation, the Court, for some, has assumed the role of guardian of the democratic consensus on the paramount importance of the rights of the individual. The question, of course, is that raised by Hand's insistence on the need for respect for precedent, the possibility that what is presented as an expansive reading of the Bill of Rights is not a Protestant interpretation but a heresy, not democratic principle but aristocratic corruption.

II

The Warren Court is known as the bench which produced *Brown v. Board of Education,* but, from today's perspective, the impact of that decision in terms of effective social change remains unclear. We are agreed on the goal of a desegregated society, and in this important sense the Warren Court has shaped the national character; lack of agreement on how to achieve that goal – indeed, even on what that goal entails – means, however, that the actual impact of *Brown* on our society remains unclear.

The law produced by *Brown* was a reading of the Fourteenth Amendment that made the Bill of Rights law for the States, but *Brown* itself reached no result at all. The question what the decision in fact meant, its impact on the communities it governed, was left to be determined in a later opinion, and it is this situation which constitutes the paradox of *Brown*. If *Brown* is attractive, it is not because of the result reached, but because it stands for inclusive community, for faith that free individuals are not inconsistent with a stable community, a goal that requires the cooperation (at a minimum) of all three branches of the federal government.

Such cooperation has not been forthcoming in large part because of the American attitude towards politics. Politics for Americans, in part because the national political parties are simply quadrennial coalitions among fifty state organizations, is a competitive activity, a contest in which what you stand for is one of the elements – and not necessarily the most important one – in whether you win or lose. It was John F. Kennedy's campaign for the White House that was most openly based on this perception of American politics. The crucial importance of appearances was an obvious truth for a campaign that succeeded in making the nation aware of a non-existent "missile gap," an Administration that openly treated its making of history as theater, that regarded effective policy as something accepted by its constituency as the simultaneous discovery and conquest of a New Frontier.

The Cuban Missile Crisis was the highpoint of the Kennedy Administration's direction of United States foreign policy, and the image produced by those days of tension is that of U.S. Ambassador Adlai Stevenson on television, confronting Russian Ambassador Zorin with aerial photographs of the missile sites. The confrontation occurred during Security Council arguments in which the Russian position was that the missiles, if they existed at all, were defensive in nature, thereby making the blockade imposed by the United States a violation of Cuba's right to self-defense and independence. "Finally, Mr. Zorin," said Stevenson, "I remind you that the other day you did not deny the existence of these weapons. Instead, we heard that they had suddenly become defensive weapons. But today – again, if I heard you correctly – you say that they do not exist, or that we have not proved they exist – and you say this with another fine flood of rhetorical scorn. All right, sir, let me ask you one simple question: do you, Ambassador Zorin, deny that the U.S.S.R. has placed and is placing medium – and intermediate-range missiles and sites in Cuba? Yes or no? Do not wait for the interpretation. Yes or no?"

Zorin said, "I am not in an American court of law, and therefore do not wish to answer a question put to me in the manner of a prosecuting counsel. You will receive the answer in due course in my capacity as representative of the Soviet Union."

Stevenson replied, "You are in the courtroom of world opinion right now, and you can answer 'Yes' or 'No.' You have denied that they exist – and I want to know whether I have understood you correctly."

Zorin said, "Please continue your statement, Mr. Stevenson. You will receive the answer in due course."

And Stevenson delivered the line that testifies to the validity of the perception of politics as theater: "I am prepared to wait for my answer until hell freezes over, if that is your decision. I am also prepared to present the evidence in this room."

Stevenson's presentation made irrelevant Zorin's argument that the metaphor of the courtroom was inappropriate; it was a sense of theater, of the impact of the "hell freezing over" phrase, that transformed a question about the "defensive" nature of the missiles into an indictment of the aggressor attempting to upset a stable balance of power. Reality as theater, moreover, was a perception that had its impact on private as well as public life in the sixties. It was the loosening of social constraints, the rejection of respectability, that was celebrated during the decade inaugurated by Kennedy's election; and Zorin was not alone in denying to law the place it once had held. The sixties, in other words, saw a rejection of law as determinative, not only by Marxists in the courtroom of public opinion, but also by American youth in the domestic arena, by the members of a society in which the Supreme Court had relied on respect for the law to be sufficient to make possible the effective implementation of its decision in *Brown v. Board of Education.*

Against this background, what we perceive as the Warren Court is most accurately summarized as an attitude that treated the meaning of law as synonymous with the right result, a treatment of judicial activity as nothing more complex or ambiguous than an attempt to do the best one can in achieving the goal of justice. To some extent, it is this attitude, the fact that *Brown* was followed by decisions dealing with reapportionment, obscenity, libel, and criminal rights, that permitted state governments and the other branches of the federal government to be less than whole-hearted in pursuing the processes of affirmative action; and from this perspective, it is *Roe v. Wade* that (although a Burger Court ruling) represents the final expression of the Warren Court.

Webster v. Reproductive Health Services held that the law made by *Roe v. Wade* governing the right to an abortion would be worked out in state legislatures and a series of forthcoming Supreme Court decisions – in short, by the processes of law. *Webster* is a decision that differs from *Brown* precisely as *Marbury v. Madison* differed from *Brown*. The right at issue in *Marbury* was accepted by the Court as legitimate, the right to receive a commission to which one was entitled. In *Marbury*, the Supreme Court refused to act. It found unconstitutional the attempt by Congress to grant it the power to act, the power to mandamus officials of a co-ordinate branch of government. In *Brown*, the Court interpreted the Constitution as requiring affirmative action, and the second *Brown* decision attempted to implement that requirement, aware that the help of the other two branches might well be needed.

Webster, like *Marbury* and unlike *Brown*, refuses to enforce a right, and it does so because, again unlike *Brown*, it interprets the federal nature of the society for which it is making law as requiring that, in connection with decisions concerning the implementation even of Constitutional rights, state as opposed to federal authorities are often legitimately entitled to have the last word. *Webster*, in short, is a decision about the role properly played by federal judicial authority in the governance of our polity; and the first *Brown* decision can thus be seen in historical perspective as an attempt by the Court to perform a task assigned by the Constitution to all three branches.

Whether this constituted corruption or courage only the future – the respect accorded the Court's decisions by those yet to come – will tell.

III

When John F. Kennedy ran against Eisenhower, his goal was clear: to become the first Catholic President of the United States. Once in office, it was not clear that Kennedy was any more efficient at persuading Congress to support forward-looking policy than Eisenhower had been. It was only in Dallas, on November 22, 1963, that the myth of Camelot, a retrospective judgment on the Thousand Days, came into being.

Camelot is a myth considerably more realistic than that embodied in *The Republic*. Like the Republic, Camelot portrays both a person and a community, but the Form that is the Republic is governed perfectly. In Camelot, on the other hand, the philosopher-king is supplanted by a band of brothers, some better than others, some weak, but all engaged in a war against evil, all aspiring to achieve the state embodied in the myth of the perfect knight.

The truth embodied in the story of Camelot is a truth embodied in the separation of powers, the belief that a good monarch is simply *primus inter pares*, and it is this truth which is essential to an understanding of the Magna Charta, a document that, like the United States Constitution, attempts to define effective freedom. The barons who demanded concrete freedoms from their monarch were aristocrats, descendants of those who had triumphed in combat, members of families whose social and political status derived from the feudal translation of personal obligation into political power. The monarchy, the feudal family that assumed a leadership role, cut the Gordian feudal knot in terms of which personal relationships were synonymous with power by insisting on a distinction between feelings of personal loyalty and the reality of public power.

The Founding Fathers of the United States worked out the consequences of that demand in terms of governmental structure; they insisted on a functional separation of powers which made unlikely agreement on a single overriding goal for the society, thus denying to government the powers claimed (and responsibilities borne) by the monarch. In fact, however, by eliminating the monarch, the Founding Fathers eliminated the symbolic repository for all of the individual oaths of fealty that had once constituted the bases for political power. As chief executive officer, the President is limited by institutions fulfilling legislative and judicial functions, and much of the power being exercised comes from the President's role as head of state and head of the political party that elected him or her to office.

In the United States, in other words, because the "fit" between the functional role and the institution, as well as that between the person and the office, is so loose, the boundary between history and myth – the discrepancy between the theoretical and actual powers of the presidency – is constantly shifting. Thus, the system of United States government is such that, come what may, John F. Kennedy would no longer have been President in 1969, and possibly not even in

1965. The paradox is that the events of November 22nd have become the starting point for new myths because the American version of the myth of Camelot both began and ended on that day in 1963.

The line between public power and personal obligation – the line whose existence is ignored by the band of brothers who populated Camelot – is the line between politics and economics in American ideology. The market which dominates United States political discourse is not only free but also posits an interaction among individuals whose only obligation is to themselves. The Japanese, although they believe themselves to possess democratic political institutions and a market economy, refuse to recognize any such line or any such market. Japanese society is devoted to efficiency, a devotion not restricted to the economic side of the line.

Thus, Japanese politics are not subject to the inefficiencies produced by a process in which power is shared by parties with different political goals, either functionally – as in a government in which legislative, executive, and judicial powers are rigidly separated – or temporally, as when opposing parties rotate control of the governmental machinery. Japanese politics are free because they permit the vote, and because that freedom carries with it the theoretical possibility that the government will change hands. The practical reality is that factions within the ruling Liberal Democratic party compete for control, but so long as Japanese voters accept Liberal Democratic goals as consonant with their own political views, it seems somehow less than conclusive that those factions are defined in terms of personal obligations while United States political parties are distinguished by political platforms that are sources of controversy every four years.

Similarly, on the economic side of the line, the Japanese have antitrust laws and competition among corporations. They are said to have an unfairly "closed" economy to which their rejoinder is that they abide by the international obligations imposed on them. Their economy is perceived as closed because the Japanese dedication to efficiency means that their antitrust laws are not enforced in situations where the competition that would result could be perceived as destructive. The question, therefore, is why, unlike the United States, Japanese society treats competition as an instrumental as opposed to substantive value.

One answer is historical, the fact that economic corporations in England and America represent private as opposed to public power, economic power controlled by individual shareholders as opposed to government power translated into state corporations and mercantilist politics. Japanese trading companies, on the other hand, are private mercantilist organizations, organizations in which the line between politics and economics is treated as formal rather than substantive, as a matter that dictates how a policy is implemented rather than how a social goal is defined.

Another answer is cultural; the Japanese accept that any structure for entrepreneurial activity is necessarily a social imposition, and hence define an effective community as one that consciously plans to obtain what it wants from a market. The Japanese, in other words, refuse to ennoble the individual, to leave the decision as to what the economy produces wholly to the consumer. These cultural differences are produced by an educational system which informs every Japanese pupil that they occupy territory too poor and too crowded to make possible the luxury of acting on the romantic view of community, a preference for individual freedom as opposed to social efficiency.

Art, both for Japan and for the United States, is an attempt to portray the emotional states produced by that with which we identify and to which we can therefore attribute meaning when we describe it. The Japanese accept the ritualistic sign which identifies an emotional state as itself real, rather than as the symbol of a reality "out there" or "in here." Japanese society, in other words, treats emotion, what feels right, as a matter of craft, to be expressed in terms of such signs, rather than as a goal to be achieved, the craft being a cultural imperative, a matter of everyday routine rather than an exceptional, spiritual truth. United States society, on the other hand, as demonstrated by the Bill of Rights, treats as truth the individual's perception, a perspective most easily grasped as the search for meaning, the attempt to assign rational significance to the events that constitute one's life, the lonely construct known as spiritual truth.

Neither choice can be imposed on any individual once they become aware of the alternative. The question for the lawyer, therefore, is the particular combination of the two that defines oneself, both the lawyer and that with which the lawyer is identified, the one that permits content with the art that has been created, the law that has been imposed on the client.

Judging, the Civil War and the Common Law
A. Holmes, Law and the Civil War

I

The courts on which Holmes sat were granted power because the inhabitants of Massachusetts and the United States believed that power corrupts, that only countervailing power could safeguard the persons subject to power, and that what was therefore required was the mixture of cooperation and competition known as federalism and checks and balances. That system faced its most severe test in the Civil War, and it was Holmes' participation in that conflict which led him to derive his view of reality from Darwinian rather than economic certainties, to treat war rather than trade as the process in terms of which humans realized themselves.

Strikingly, however, Holmes' description of war rests on acceptance of a religious rather than scientific certainty, on invocation of the long run, that state of affairs defined, to paraphrase Keynes, as the time when we shall all be dead. "War, when you are in it, is horrible and dull. It is only when time has passed that you can see that its message was divine. I hope it may be long before we are called again to sit at that master's feet. But some teacher of the kind we all need."

Finally to assess Holmes, therefore, requires an assessment of the Civil War, the conflict that made him the judge he was and that thus provided an attitude towards law that made him an icon, someone who represented the judge as the United States desired him or her to be.

II

On August 23, 1864, Abraham Lincoln had his Cabinet members sign the outside of a sealed memorandum in which he had written: "This morning, as for some days past, it seems exceedingly probable that this Administration will not be re-elected. Then it will be my duty to so co-operate with the President elect [George B. McClellan], as to save the Union between the election and the inauguration; as he will have secured his election on such ground that he cannot possibly save it afterwards." Lincoln's prediction was based on the fact that, after three years of warfare, Union troops, although victories had been won, seemed once again to have been stalemated by Confederate armies that seemed unwilling to admit defeat. McClellan in a way symbolized the forces underlying Lincoln's prognosis.

While Union troops were losing the first battle at Bull Run, McClellan was winning victories in West Virginia. Called to the rescue of a capital city that felt threatened by the possibility of falling to enemy forces, McClellan rebuilt a shattered army, but seemed incapable of winning decisive victories with it, a pattern that eventually led Lincoln to dismiss him on November 8, 1862.

Events following his dismissal demonstrated the extent to which he had forged an identification with his Army of the Potomac. Burnside, who succeeded him as commander of that force, was believed to be a popular commander. Demoralization was so complete, however, that he eventually resigned when Lincoln refused to dismiss or transfer the eight generals whom Burnside blamed for his lack of success. Morale rose under Burnside's successor, Hooker, but Lincoln replaced him with Meade in June, 1863, justifying the transition to his cabinet on the basis that Hooker had turned out to be another McClellan.

In the spring of 1864, Lincoln appointed Grant general in chief (a role McClellan had played in addition to his Army command), and lieutenant general, a rank revived by Congress and previously held only by George Washington and Winfield Scott. Grant designated Sherman as his successor in command of western armies, and came east to make his headquarters with the Army of the Potomac. Although Meade remained in command of this force, its cavalry was put under the command of Sheridan.

These generals eventually won the Civil War, and, as a result, McClellan's story has become part of the myth of Lincoln as a successor to George Washington, savior of the nation created by his predecessor, who understood that Grant was a fighter, someone who could use the Army created by McClellan, not only to save Washington, but to bring the South back into the Union. To the extent that that myth is accurate, it makes incomprehensible the unsuccessful impeachment of Lincoln's successor. If what the Union needed was victory, why was Reconstruction necessary? If, on the other hand, victory was insufficient, on what basis did Lincoln find McClellan inadequate?

III

That McClellan was not committed to the proposition of attack, of taking the battle to the enemy, is clear. He regularly overestimated both the numbers and the prowess of the opposing forces, thus permitting the Confederates to take great tactical risks, he was a trainer and administrator as opposed to a battlefield leader, and, when victory eluded him, he evaded the responsibility by blaming those for whom he was fighting: "I have lost all regard and respect for the majority of the administration and doubt the propriety of my brave men's blood being shed to further the designs of such a set of heartless villains."

Lincoln's military strategy was based on his appreciation of the North's material superiority, his theory being that constant attack would necessarily wear the Confederates down. In general terms, this is, of course, both obvious and unassailable, but war is a matter of concrete particulars, of tactics as much as strategy, morale as well as material and timing as well as odds. As we learned in Vietnam, moreover, people who perceive themselves as defending their own property against foreign invaders can defy rational calculations over long stretches of time.

The Vietnam conflict, of course, took place a century after the Civil War, but it was not only McClellan who felt that the principle of constant attack was an insufficient basis on which to conduct the campaign against the Confederates. On September 1st, shortly after McClellan was nominated for the Presidency by the Democratic Party, the city of Atlanta fell to Sherman's army. Thereafter, Sherman persuaded Grant, and Grant Lincoln, that what was required was a new type of warfare, a strategy of devastation rather than attack. As Sherman put it to the mayor of Atlanta in justifying the order expelling that city's civilian population, "War is cruelty and you cannot refine it." "[W]hen peace does come, you may call on me for anything," but, until then, "we are not fighting hostile armies, but a hostile people, and must make old and young, rich and poor, feel the hard hand of war."

The politics underlying supervision of McClellan's conduct of the war were, however, by no means as focused as Sherman on the need for victory. Congressional committees, for example, obtained testimony from generals subordinate to McClellan disagreeing both with his political views and his military strategy. Similarly, Lincoln at one point refused to take sides in a public dispute between McClellan and Stanton, the Secretary of War, telling a rally only that the quarrel was not really as deep as those pretending to be their friends said it was. Politics and war, in short, were not easy to separate because it was not yet regarded as inappropriate publicly to acknowledge the overlap between the two.

IV

Analyses of the relationship between Lincoln and McClellan often focus on the arrogance of the latter and the forbearance of the former, the general condescending to the president, going to bed despite the fact that his chief executive is waiting for an interview, revealing to a reporter military plans he refused to share with his commander-in-chief. McClellan, on this analysis, is wholly explicable as a victim of his own success. Second in his class at West Point, chief engineer and vice-president of a railroad at 30 and president two years later, he responds not to reality, but to the demands of an oversize ego. Thus, when Lincoln noted the "vast labor" involved in being general commanding the war effort as well as commander of a field army, McClellan's reply was "I can do it all."

On this analysis, the difference between Lincoln and McClellan was that one was in touch with reality, while the other was an egoist deceived by his own ability to succeed. McClellan, after all, did not in fact replace Lincoln as President. The soldiers he had once led, moreover, voted against him by a considerably greater margin than the electorate in general. Even the Army of the Potomac, it seems, perceived something in Lincoln that was missing in its creator.

McClellan was slow to take the offensive because of his belief in the virtues of the "set piece" battle. "It has always been my opinion that the true course in conducting military operations is to make no movement until the preparations are as complete as circumstances permit, and never to fight a battle without some definite object worth the probable loss." His preparations made him popular because his troops fought infrequently and only from positions of superior strength. The gap between his strategy and that of Lincoln, therefore, arose because of a disagreement about the "worth [of] the probable loss," and the party platform on which he ran for president made clear the difference in the "objects" for which Lincoln and McClellan believed the Civil War was being fought.

McClellan, like Lincoln prior to the Emancipation Proclamation, felt that a war fought solely to restore the Union, rather than to abolish slavery, was justified. For McClellan, the issue was one of principle rather than politics. He made only two public appearances during the Presidential campaign. The basis for his political disagreement with his president was spelled out in a speech he gave at West Point in June, before he had been nominated by the Democratic

Party. The occasion was the dedication of a site honoring those who had fallen in a conflict whose origins he ascribed to extremists on both sides, men "with whom sectional and personal prejudices and interests outweighed all considerations for the general good."

Lincoln, of course, would not disagree that those who rule should prefer the general good to narrower interests. Lincoln's objection, the basis for his prediction that McClellan as President "[could] not possibly save [the Union]," was that the slogan of the Copperhead faction of the Democratic party, the group that wanted peace at any price, was "The Constitution as it is, the Union as it was." For Lincoln, in other words, the Thirteenth Amendment had already been written.

Thus, the basis on which McClellan ran for the Presidency was that "we should exhaust all the resources of statesmanship . . . to secure . . . peace, reestablish the Union, and guarantee for the future the Constitutional rights of every state." On the surface, these were not goals with which Lincoln could disagree. The disagreements, rather, were about the measures that had already been taken, measures justified as necessary to effective conduct of the war.

On September 24, 1862, Lincoln suspended the right to habeas corpus and substituted military trial for persons accused of disloyalty or interference with recruitment for the military. Two days earlier, a preliminary draft of the Emancipation Proclamation had been disclosed, and McClellan was not alone in conflating the two, "the recent Proclamations of the Presdt inaugurating servile war, emancipating the slaves, and at one stroke of the pen changing our free institutions into a despotism – for such I regard as the natural effect of the last Proclamation suspending the Habeas Corpus throughout the land."

In December, the House of Representatives, on a party line vote, defeated a Democratic resolution branding emancipation "a high crime against the Constitution." If Lincoln was a better leader than McClellan, therefore, it is because the idea of "[t]he Constitution as it is" is a chimera, an ideal or goal rather than a reality, because Lincoln was "in tune" with his times in a sense McClellan was not.

V

Lincoln, in his campaign for President and during his terms in office, completed the Jacksonian revolution – which created political parties as we know them – by presiding over development of a political party which justified withdrawing constitutional privileges on the basis that such actions were a necessary means to ends which were a matter of morality rather than ideology, neutral truths rather than partisan rationalizations. In military terms, the result was the replacement of McClellan, who felt it proper to insist on what he felt to be right, with Grant, who, like Sherman, analyzed victory as a question of military efficiency rather than political principle, thus leaving the question of war aims to the processes of Reconstruction. In historical terms, a stress on efficiency enabled the United States to undertake both the processes of industrialization and imperialistic military adventures.

In connection with law, on the other hand, the cultural transformation produced by the Civil War created a definitive split between the Constitution and the Supreme Court, the opinions of the Justices and the Constitution as it should be. Reading the Thirteenth

Amendment into the Constitution prior to its enactment is not the only example of this transformation, since, in connection with *Dred Scott*, the Supreme Court decision that defined slaves as property rather than legal persons, Lincoln could abide by the law precisely by treating it in a technically correct manner as a decision applicable only to the persons who were involved in the litigation which produced the opinion.

The problem with such a position is, of course, the extent to which it makes the work of the Court impossible, destroying the concept of precedent, the concept which makes law both powerful and efficient by embodying the premise that things "fit," that the propositions in terms of which we rule ourselves are connected in ways we can rationally comprehend, that the Platonic Form exists. The Civil War, in short, replaced law with force, and the political decision to make abolition of slavery a war aim as opposed to a matter of law after peace had been restored thus made Reconstruction not only necessary but also likely not to succeed; and it made of law a principled nuisance with which the man who became a judicial icon had to contend once he assumed his seat on the bench.

VI

In a letter dated October 27, 1912, Holmes analyzes his motivation as a writer, both of law and about law:

> "The only thing that charms my fancy is to know a thing as a master and to put into it some fundamental ideas, that the public won't know enough to give you credit for – that you are lucky if you get any credit for it, but that if your dream is true [your ideas] are first rate and shaping. Then to carry your theory and attitude into

detail and practice and thus to submit it to the test of reality is the other half. But is not the big thing to show the infinite in the finite? To take some detail that presents itself as mere arbitrary fact and to show it as a case of the universal?"

This analysis makes clear that Holmes, like Socrates, has set himself the goal of capturing the Form, the essence of the phenomenon, that unifying substance or process which underlies the appearances – those adaptations to specific circumstances – which we encounter in our daily lives. Holmes' opinions, however, work like all good literature, as works of art, utilizing the vivid image, not to verify an empirical proposition, but to appeal to emotions, confirming our felt certainties about how we know things should be, committing us, not to a rational result but to an emotionally satisfying conclusion. .

Holmes, moreover, in part no doubt because of his experience in the Civil War, is not only an artist, but also a cynic, someone who agrees that Socrates may have been asking relevant questions, but denies that the search for answers has a meaning, that potential relevance is a sufficient basis for faith. Hand, unlike Holmes, is not skeptical about precedent, which defines relevance in the law, and this faith was, for Hand, fully as functional a philosophy as the scientific faith that the form of electro-magnetic energy known as light can be treated as having a constant speed. That c is a constant, however, is a truth social in nature, shared by the community of scientists, whereas faith in a pattern of precedent is, like all spiritual truth, an individual matter, acceptance of being what one is, someone who believes in the law, who denies Holmes' scientific truth that law is applied politics.

The question that remains, therefore, is the nature of the common law, the mystery that encompasses both the cynic and the man of faith.

B. Judges, Philosophy and the Common Law
I

Style is the manifestation of one's culture, the expression of one's emotional makeup, the mood in terms of which one's activities are conducted; and Cardozo's style is the conceit that one can be transparent about style, can treat the perspective one brings to reality as itself a matter one can control as opposed to a given that must be accepted. Cardozo's opinions are effective because, in reading them, one cannot distinguish style from substance; and the consequence is that they become precedents *for themselves*, cited for principles that may or may not be applied to the dispute being adjudicated. Holmes' opinions, on the other hand, like those written by Hand, are adjudications, concrete decisions that can be accepted or distinguished in deciding the case before the court.

Cardozo, in short, is seen as seeking justice and doing equity, as declaring principles valid whatever the particular facts, because he demonstrates that he is in control of the law he is responsible for making in the sense that Cardozo's law is indistinguishable from equity. Unfortunately, this means that Cardozo's opinions are not social, in that they afford future judges no basis on which to determine whether the decision is a justification or rationalization for the result. Thus, equity in fact functions as the "politics" of law, the recognition of "special" interests, of reasons to introduce inefficiency into the system.

The limit law necessarily places on the doing of equity is, therefore, the limit economics places on politics, recognition of the commonality that may underlie human diversity, the hope that not all values conflict, that personal cultures are at least partially congruent. His opinions afford us no way of telling whether Cardozo observes that limit.

II

Hand lacked both Holmes' and Cardozo's mastery of law because he understood that the making of common law involves the possibility of the sin of pride, of attempting to impose one's own beliefs on the litigants whose dispute is being adjudicated. Thus, a judge's conscious values can be incompatible with federalism, a system designed to permit the co-existence of potentially conflicting value systems, and which therefore assumes on the part of government officials the spiritual willingness to accept evil as well as good. Even apart from considerations of federalism, a common law judge in his or her work necessarily confronts the issue that separates Hand and Cardozo, the nature of the respect demanded by the social need for stability embodied in the concept of the precedent.

Precedent is the mechanism that enables the judge to resist the demands of his or her own feelings, to transcend their personal version of cultural and political ideology, but it inevitably involves a focus on the past. The problem, therefore, is the art of making new law, and the answer to that mystery is that Holmes and Cardozo are successful in making new law precisely because, as artists, they are *not* humble, because they dare to be certain about the existence of legal answers. If it is objected that this lack of humility involves treating others as means rather than ends, the response would be that recognizing such a possibility is recognizing law as applied *Realpolitik*, and that Hand is neither realistic insofar as he treats precedent as a substantive rather than formal truth nor a skeptic insofar as that attitude towards precedent is a matter of faith rather than philosophy.

Holmes' certainty in writing his opinions is the negative truth that one gains from cynicism. The contrast with the positive truth of faith – Hand's reliance on precedent, his trust in a professional formality – raises the fundamental philosophical question inherent in the work of Plato and Aristotle. A Form for Socrates (and Plato) was an ultimate sort of truth. Socrates and Plato made no distinction between science and art, and they did not make an explicit connection between art (which they feared) and the death of Socrates; but the latter's trial made clear that Socrates submitted to the judgment of the court because he derived his notion of justice from a Form and that Forms make it impossible to draw a distinction between truth and personal interpretation.

Aristotle replaced the Form with a focus on process, on how things are done, a shift that enables one to distinguish the work of art that attempts to evoke emotion from the experiment that attempts to prove the existence of a scientific fact. Plato's objection would have been that this distinction was not ethically functional, in that it did not inform humans how they should behave. Aristotle's response – had they been using today's language – would be that focusing on human process involves focusing on emotions, and that emotions – as opposed to abstract ethical principles – determine our behavior.

Plato and Aristotle could not have this exchange because they shared a belief system that did not distinguish the scientific facts which for Holmes constituted truth from emotions, a system which enabled Socrates to reason that the Form of justice – the judgment of the court – was itself truth. Such a belief system may seem simplistic, but it creates the cultural homogeneity assumed by Rousseau when he developed the concept of General Will, a concept that uses the possibility of personal determination, of willing something, to postulate the existence of a community consensus.

General Will makes the power exercised by a government legitimate, but most nations – including the national citizenry created by the Constitution subscribed to by the colonies that constituted the United States of America – do not possess the homogeneity assumed by Rousseau. The cultural homogeneity assumed by Rousseau makes the Platonic Form a plausible concept, and Hegel dealt with the fact of cultural diversity by systematizing Aristotle's focus on process.

Culture, for Hegel, is a synthesis of potentially contradictory forces he denominated theses and antitheses. A synthesis is a shift in perspective from the chronologically prior synthesis, thus revealing the eternal antinomies – good and evil, God and the Devil, truth and falsehood – in a new light. The fact that cultures change does not, however, justify the conclusion that theses and antitheses – the Hegelian version of Platonic Forms – in fact exist. That question is the question whether our universe is ultimately orderly rather than chaotic in character, and the answer to that question is a matter of faith rather than philosophy.

III

How does one tell the truth about the law and thus reveal what the law really is?

One can succumb to the temptation to be authoritative, to derive the correct result from the formula, to characterize the equitable exception as part of the system defined by the legal rule, to insist that the process is explicable. With luck (or grace or providence), one will avoid being faced with the hard case with which one's view of the legal system cannot deal; and thus one will be capable of bringing technical precision to bear on the telling of the truth.

Is being authoritative proper, or is it ignoring the truth contained in the hard case? Critical legal studies began as an attack on the coercive nature of Socratic dialogue, and that attack was based on the assumption that the hard case can be ignored, that the sole purpose of law is to teach the correct result. Thus, Socratic dialogue, which prior to the sixties was the basis for legal education, is coercive insofar as the questioner relies on the assumption that an answer to the question exists; and law is the system that operates "as if" the question it defines at trial can be answered. The proposition that the "as if" has a connection with truth is, however, a matter of faith.

Critical Legal Studies treats the hard case as the product of political ideology, a manifestation of totalitarianism. Critical Legal Studies, in short, was made possible by World War II, the successful crusade against totalitarianism. That crusade was both based on and productive of the oxymoronic belief that American culture was non-ideological and yet provided bases for action, a belief that reconciles law with equity, the free market with the need for antitrust laws to ensure the continued existence of competition.

The non-ideological ideology is not that antitrust laws are rules rather than regulation. The belief, rather, is that they are laws rather than authoritarian politics, that laws are somehow rational or reasonable in a way politics is not. One way of describing this distinction is to say that laws are accepted as legitimate in a way that political (or administrative) decisions are not, that the law is perceived as a product of the consensus that makes democratic government possible, that the law *is* that consensus, the goal politics is designed to achieve, as distinguished from the power at work in the political process itself.

World War II was followed by the Cold War, and the need to carry on the crusade against a former ally was rationalized by a similar distinction, a version of the American cultural myth that, in personal terms, one is free to define one's future, and, in political terms, that democracy is the antithesis of totalitarianism because democracy is in a topographical sense midway between the right and left versions of the same thing, the totalitarianism that is produced by Nazi and Communist ideologies. The Hitler phenomenon, however, was not the "right" version of the political ideology of Communism (a designation applicable, if at all, only to the corporate fascism propounded by Mussolini), but rather an exercise in cultural nostalgia, the replacement of the democratic mechanism by the individual leader.

Hitler's speeches were triumphs, not of the rhetoric of political or cultural ideology, but of the power of emotion, not of reason, but of will, celebrations of the replacement of the compromises and sacrifices inherent in democratic consensus by a will that presented itself as sufficiently powerful to control the future. The Third Reich's totalitarianism can thus be understood as political power exercised without the restraints embodied in the unarticulated, because social, ideology known as culture, as politics *per se* – *Realpolitik* – rather than the applied politics contained in the common law judicial system.

Common, as opposed to civil, law embodies that freedom to define one's own future, that liberty, which characterizes American cultural and political ideologies. Courts in both civil and common law countries look to the purpose of the statute in determining whether or not the law is applicable to a given set of facts, but the cultural presumptions underlying that interpretive process differ markedly. Civil law is treated as a system, meaning that, if you cannot do something in the way the statute prescribes, the statute can be read as barring you from doing it, thus encouraging the perception that actions not falling within the statute are by definition illegitimate. In a common law jurisdiction, statutes are treated as attempts to regulate otherwise legitimate activities, thus permitting the argument that prohibitions not falling within the statute's purpose are by definition illegitimate.

The ultimate question, however, is why the directives contained in the statutes should be obeyed, why the law should be treated as legitimate, and the answer is that American culture treats common law precedents as attempts to do equity – decisions on the basis of all relevant facts whether or not statutes or precedents should be applied –

as well as attempts to apply existing law to a new situation. The ultimate legal questions, therefore, are constitutional ones: the sort of government entitled to exercise power in a capitalist democratic state and the limits on that power.

My philosophy asserts that cultures differ in their temporal perspectives, whether what is important is tomorrow, next year or eternity. Do you agree? If not, why not? If so, was the difference between Athens and Sparta that the latter lived in the present whereas Athens, because its inhabitants were not all dedicated to a single goal – the winning of wars – had to define its character by distinguishing the past from the future? If not, why not? If so, is the difference between Lenin and Hitler as historical actors that the former created a party that was trying to achieve Athens and the latter one which achieved Sparta?

CHAPTER 3:
POWER AND CULTURE

Analyzing Capitalist Democracy

I

The ideals that energize United States politics energized the religious rebels known as Puritans, as well as the varied groups of immigrants who followed them, all of whom had in common choosing to leave their societies of origin. Our times are interesting because those immigrant ideals are now spreading to the societies of origin, where populations watch television programs produced in the United States while political leaders attempt to create the infrastructure which consultants inform them is required by a democratic capitalist culture.

This transformation is perceived by Americans as the triumph of democratic capitalism, the emergence of civil societies from totalitarian or authoritarian rule. Such a perception overlooks the fact that civil society is no more than a term that designates a non-totalitarian state, a world in which the political (party) organization does not claim authority to direct (without opposition) all economic and social activity; and treating civil society as a real category denoting non-political (i.e., social and economic) human activities reveals the extent to which democratic capitalism is indeed peculiarly American, rooted in the Utopian biases of the Enlightenment. The Enlightenment was the period when cultural power became democratic, when the need for the individual to accept secular and ecclesiastical authority was questioned by the holders of such authority, thus making plausible a society energized by the goal of freedom from constraint, political ideals with which religious rebels would feel comfortable.

An enlightened society ascribes to the law that ability to control social and economic activities which has historically been exercised by secular and ecclesiastical authority. The English monarchs used the bureaucracies in which that secular and ecclesiastical authority was embodied to develop those institutions of law and equity which shifted power from feudal magnates first to the monarchy and ultimately to the law; and, in the United States, the Warren Court (one of the three separate but equal branches into which royal power had evolved) promulgated the doctrine that the Constitutional Bill of Rights made freedom from constraint a governmental goal. What renders this evolution Utopian is the existence of culture, the fact that the elements of stability and cohesion that define a society require humans to behave as socialized creatures, to in effect restrain themselves. Thus, law is not only justice, a charter of freedom from arbitrary power, but also applied politics, an attempt to control human behavior; and the United States Bill of Rights embodies plausible restraints only insofar as the framers intended such absolute restraints to apply to the central as opposed to state governments.

Marxism promulgated the doctrine that the constraints produced by politics could be eliminated by creating the proper social and economic environment. Humans, however, recognize at least three different forms of power; and Marx confused the first and third, thus enabling him to ignore the second. Scientific power is knowledge, the ability to predict the configuration resulting from, or the path taken by, the activities of the entities we believe constitute the material world. Spiritual power is produced by serenity, the ability to accept the things we cannot change, which enables us to focus on the ability to change the things we can, to make ourselves what we believe some persons can be, to conform to ideals we feel overestimate the capacities of human nature. Political power is social in nature, based on relationships among members of a society and exemplified by patterns of behavior that are compatible with the existence of an acknowledged ordering of those members.

Political power is something we learn about in our cribs, when we become conscious of the fact that certain behaviors produce results which are pleasing to us, a sequence of events we associate with the physical strength that permits us to order our material environment. The problem raised by that discovery is the potential awareness it carries with it of the dual nature of conscious political behavior, the fact that we function both as a participant in the community known as the family and, to the extent that we are conscious, as an observer of the behaviors that create that community. Insofar as we are acting in our observer role, we attempt to learn the community's culture, the rules that govern proper behavior, to become the person we want to be, a situation that may involve choosing to participate in a community incompatible with our family's culture. Insofar as we are acting as a participant in a given culture, our participation is most clearly delineated as establishing a price, what it is you are willing to give up and what you expect in return.

Put this way, what makes democratic capitalism (and the concept of culture) utopian is the need for faith, the faith that the rationality embodied in the market paradigm is an accurate description of human behavior. Thus, as all students of the stock market understand, there are two basic ways of analyzing market behavior. Fundamentalists believe that knowledge is power, and seek to correlate market behavior with what the given fundamentalist believes to be the important factor or factors. Chartists believe that the process is its own determinant, and seek to ascertain regularities without necessarily correlating them with any extraneous factor. Each method, of course, acknowledges that, under some circumstances, the other is more appropriate, but neither is capable of indicating in advance when its own method will cease to be relevant. What neither method can incorporate is that knowledge, like political power and spirituality, is ultimately a matter of mysteries (or statistically verifiable odds) humans cannot completely comprehend, an insight the Enlightenment would have dismissed as a rationalization for the ecclesiastical tyranny from which it hoped to free the world.

II

Human culture responds to the fact of mortality, or, to be precise, attempts to deny the functional significance of that fact, to establish the proposition that the behaviors engaged in by members of the relevant culture or sub-culture have a meaning other than that of preparing for departure from the world in which one lives. Participation in cultures in personal terms takes the form of resonances, awareness that things, "fit" or "feel right" or are "as they should be."

Such resonances are conceptualized as emotions, things we know are real, but which change so quickly and for such a variety of reasons that they provide models for the existence of the philosophical concept known as the Platonic Form.

The reward for mastering a culture can be the ability to lead, to be an entrepreneur or a manager, both of whom direct other people's political, social, and/or economic activities. Managers have that ability because they are recognized either as having power (by election or appointment to office or by purchase or inheritance) or as possessing the prudence and competence that incorporate the values embodied in the community's culture. Entrepreneurs know how a given activity should be undertaken, and those that are successful are recognized as demonstrating that the culture requires change, that a new technology or ideology must be absorbed, or that a return to older values is required. A potential entrepreneur, in other words, is simply a technician, someone whose mastery of technique, of how something is done, may not suffice to move him or her into a higher social class, who may be denied managerial power, or whose innovation may fail to find a market.

Not every Rubicon produces a Caesar, nor every conspiracy theory a Hitler. History attempts to inform us about the unanswerable questions whether the times are made by the technician or whether the entrepreneur is shaped by his or her environment; social science is about things we can validly say when validity is defined as objective truth rather than literary resonance. Can one, therefore, define democratic capitalism in objective terms rather than as the precipitate of the history of the United States of America?

III

Our Republic was created, not because monarchs could not be benevolent, but because power tends to corrupt. The theory underlying the American revolution is that the more concentrated the institutional components of a government, the greater the chance of corruption. The moral judgment which informs this theory contrasts government by law and personal rule. Thus, the laws that attempted to tax unrepresented American colonies were passed by Parliament, but the British monarch could exercise not only executive but also legislative and judicial powers. Moreover, the fact that the Church of England was not separated from the monarchy meant that both spiritual and material sovereignty were embodied in the same person.

The goal of those who consciously subscribed to the theory was not power but fame, not the right to rule but confirmation that their rule was legitimate, the belief that following the theory meant that power could be used to create precedents worthy of emulation. The theory of our Constitution is that the Court interprets, the Congress legislates, and the President executes the law. The extent to which Washington accepted this theory is demonstrated by his refusal to choose between Jefferson and Hamilton. That he was aware of the extent to which their views diverged is clear from the efforts he made to smooth over personal differences between them. It is striking, however, that he treated his role as one involving personalities rather than the policies the two men represented, despite the fact that both Jefferson and

Hamilton actively worked with supporters both in the Congress and the press.

Washington, in short, saw the Presidency as "above" the making of policy choices, and was therefore puzzled when he was accused of monarchical tendencies. He was, after all, only executing the policies others promulgated. The function of the fame pursued by Washington, however, is legitimacy, justification for the power whose exercise is governed by the President's discretion, and that function cannot be understood except in Chartist terms, in terms of the process itself.

Thus, because fame is a functional rather than substantive goal, Washington seeks it neither for his own sake nor for the national authority created by the constituent States, but solely to make the system of government work, properly to perform his public responsibilities. Indeed, as Washington pointed out in announcing the alliance with France to the revolutionary army, fame is, in the end, the result of spiritual rather than material power: "It having pleased the Almighty ruler of the Universe propitiously to defend the Cause of the United American-States and finally by raising us up a powerful Friend among the Princes of the Earth to establish our liberty and Independence up[on] lasting foundations, it becomes us to set apart a day for gratefully acknowledging the divine goodness and celebrating the important Event which we owe to his benign Interposition."

IV

We learn politics in our cribs. Where, then, do we learn the rules of civil society, the non-political politics known to social science as the phenomenon of culture, those conscious and unconscious rules that are more binding than the formal ones known as laws, either the limits ignored by speeding automobiles, or the scientific statistics flouted by smokers?

As the victor in the battle pointed out, Waterloo was won on the playing fields of Eton, and when the New Deal attempted to justify the use of law to regulate corporate activities, the image invoked was that of the referee. It is in games, in other words, that we learn what competition means in operational terms, how to cooperate in a competitive context and how to compete, (while being cooperative), when our personal goals are as important as, and/or part of, winning the game. The better you become at playing a game, and the better the opposition, the more you learn the extent to which what you do can define what the rule is treated as requiring.

Learning how a game is played, in short, is creating a culture by participating in it. The question that concerns this course is how the community defined by that culture should be governed.

Leadership and the Party
I.

The President's power is produced by and makes effective our aspiration to be a nation. Unlike the judiciary, the President is not the symbol of renunciation of power represented by fidelity to the law. Nor does the President represent the truth that effective power is necessarily parochial because all power is local. Presidential power, rather, is justified by the fact that leadership is a necessary component of human life.

The systems of federalism and separation of powers however are designed precisely to limit the effectiveness of leadership. Franklin Roosevelt was an effective President. How he chose his successor should therefore be informative about the nature of the Presidency of the United States of America.

II

James Byrnes' term as a Supreme Court Justice was his consolation for having been denied the Democratic vice-presidential nomination in 1940. He continued, while on the Court, to serve as a bridge between Franklin Roosevelt and the Congress, in which he had achieved a leadership position in a remarkably few years.

He left the Court after little more than a Term because he was needed to oversee the economy whose productivity made victory in World War II possible, a task whose success led the Press to give him the title of Assistant President. Given that title, he was clearly in the running to replace Henry Wallace as vice-president in 1944, a time when Roosevelt's declining health made the decision about who the vice-president should be a crucial one.

The failure to nominate Byrnes in 1940 was justified by three factors: opposition from labor and civil rights organizations and concern that Byrnes' conversion from Catholicism to the Episcopal Church would prove a liability. The last of these, while it might be a deciding factor in a decision between equal contenders, does not seem determinative. Similarly, the racist charge at this point in history, while significant (since civil rights was beginning to emerge as an issue), was not itself determinative. To say that Byrnes was a segregationist is simply to acknowledge that he was a Southerner, and Southerners were still a crucial part of the Democratic Party. In political terms, in other words, civil rights was a Republican issue, and a person with qualifications as exemplary as those possessed by Byrnes therefore remained a significant candidate.

Byrnes himself saw labor opposition as his greatest hurdle, and his immediate response to being denied the 1944 nomination was to demonize the CIO executive Sidney Hillman. The Republican characterization of Franklin Roosevelt as the President who "cleared" all important decisions "with Sidney" was Byrnes' explanation (after 1944) of why he lost his bid for vice-president in 1940.

III

Less than a week before the 1944 Democratic Convention, Mayor Kelley of Chicago (a prominent Democrat) told Robert Hannegan, Chairman of the Democratic National Committee, that African-American leaders had told him (Kelley) that Roosevelt had the

African-American vote no matter who his vice-president was. Kelley knew that Hannegan would be glad to hear this since Hannegan, like many prominent Democrats, had long perceived Vice-president Wallace as a liability, a man who could not be relied on, someone who embraced causes rather than executing programs. When Hannegan repeated the news to Roosevelt, the response was that the vice-presidency was "settled", a typical Roosevelt response in that it committed him to no position at all, despite the fact that Roosevelt knew that Hannegan heard that word as an acknowledgement that Byrnes had the nomination.

At breakfast the next day, Byrnes was told by Kelley and Hannegan that Roosevelt had said "Well, you know Jimmy has been my choice from the very first" "Go ahead and name him." The fact was, however, that Kelley had either misunderstood or misrepresented the position of the African-American leaders, and later that day Edward Flynn, the Democratic boss in the Bronx who had always opposed Byrnes as someone who would lose the crucial African-American vote, arrived in Chicago; and, when he heard what had happened, called Roosevelt in San Diego and repeated his opposition. Later that same afternoon, Hannegan called San Diego to report labor's opposition, and Roosevelt withdrew his support for Byrnes' candidacy.

There was, at this point in time, circulating at the Convention, a letter from Roosevelt stating that he would be happy with either William Douglas or Harry Truman as the vice-presidential candidate, and there was also a letter stating that, if Roosevelt were a delegate to the Convention, he would support Henry Wallace. The question, therefore, is what Roosevelt was trying to accomplish, why he was refusing to lead the Convention. The answer is that Roosevelt was motivated, not by questions about the weight to be given to racial or labor matters, but by the desire to replace Henry Wallace as vice-president. His leadership style was to accomplish this by relying on the political "market" rather than taking personal responsibility for the decision arrived at.

IV

The 1944 Democratic vice-presidential decision is a paradigmatic case study in effective capitalist democratic leadership. Byrnes, from Roosevelt's point of view, was a politician like himself who bridged divergences and mediated between extremes. He was, in short, not an ideologue. In the end, however, this similarity was insufficient to persuade Roosevelt to insist on Byrnes, though Roosevelt never articulated the basis for his reluctance.

The magic of Roosevelt's leadership inheres in this willingness to leave what is most crucial a mystery, possibly even to himself. Because power is ultimately something that can only be defined in its own terms, by being possessed, its exercise necessarily involves this element of magic. The possessor knows, however, that those subject to the power must believe that the magic is explicable, that the possessor has an understanding of what is happening. How one deals with this ambiguity – how one acts – is what defines one's nature as a political leader.

The remaining question, therefore, is not what Roosevelt knew or felt, but the meaning of what he did, the assessment of the difference between the aristocrat who was president and the self-made lawyer denied the right to succeed his superior. From an objective perspective, it is clear that, in 1944, Roosevelt was denying his own mortality, refusing to take into account that the 1944 vice-president would be his successor. Only this fact explains why Harry Truman was not privy to such secrets as the existence of the atomic bomb.

V

When Byrnes lost his position as Truman's Secretary of State, Truman's decision was seen by some as the rejection of a "tough" line in negotiations with the Soviet Union. Truman's objection, however, was not to the policies espoused by Byrnes but to the fact that policy was not "cleared" with the President, that the Secretary of State was behaving as though he had the right to create that policy. Byrnes, in short, was insufficiently "political" in dealing with the man who was now his superior. The reason for this behavior is historical, the fact that, when Truman arrived at the 1944 Democratic Convention, he had in his pocket the speech he had promised to give nominating Byrnes as the vice-presidential candidate. It was as a result of this fact that it took Roosevelt a phone call to persuade Truman to accept the vice-presidential nomination and that Byrnes became Truman's Secretary of State.

Nor was the divergence between Byrnes and Truman limited to foreign affairs. After his replacement as Secretary of State, Byrnes began to oppose proposed Fair Deal legislation as both wasteful and attempts to shift power from elected state officials to federal bureaucrats. As a result, Truman characterized Byrnes as a "disloyal"

Democrat. Truman's loyalty, in other words, was to party policies, Byrnes to principle – American ideals in foreign affairs and constitutional aspirations in domestic affairs – and Roosevelt's to his role as President, to the necessity to lead. For Roosevelt, principles oversimplified the decisions facing a practitioner of the art of politics. Thus, he found it impossible to deal with de Gaulle, who refused ever to compromise what he perceived as the interests of France. Was de Gaulle's attitude in part the product of the fact that he had made himself the leader of Free France, a position he had neither inherited nor to which he was elected?

Whatever the answer to that question, the issue presented by Roosevelt's decision about the 1944 vice-presidential nomination is whether "good" politics in a democratic capitalist republic is anything more than the cynical certainty that the attempt to define one's personal responsibility oversimplifies the decision one is called upon to make, whether "good" politics are necessarily amoral. Political power is amoral when it is the end rather than the means. Are ends matters of ideology? If so, does capitalism erode the culture which defines a society's ideology? Must power be amoral once the holder ceases to be responsible for fulfilling Divine purposes?

Politics and Economics

The United States is a nation founded by revolution, a society in which separation of powers results from and in a distrust of politics while capitalism commits the society to a process of "creative destruction" of social and economic institutions. The risks involved in processes of "creative destruction," like the sacrifices of efficiency in the application of political power entailed by a system of separation of powers, are traceable to the optimistic view of human nature which characterized the thinking of the Enlightenment.

Mystery, for the Enlightenment, was obscurantism, and Kant derived the Golden Rule in a rational manner by utilizing the resources of logic and analysis. Divine truth had shifted from being a political matter of tribal might (the power that determined the outcome of combat) to becoming a personal matter of spiritual meaning, a transition which the Protestant Reformation carried through in doctrinal terms, although separation of church and state waited upon the replacement of monarchs by republics. In the absence of Divine sanction, however, the legitimacy of political power – the fact of obedience in the absence of a threat of imminent violence – becomes dependent upon a system of checks and balances that promise to protect the individual from potential abuse, upon the appearance of the version of the philosopher-king known as the benevolent despot, or upon effective totalitarian organization (meaning political structure that imposes itself on social and economic areas).

It is against this intellectual background that constitutional republics such as the United States of America are brought into being, and perhaps the best example of the impact of that background on the attitudes of politicians is provided by the attitude of President Harry S. Truman towards the Pendergast machine, which provided the monetary resources for his political campaigns.

The Pendergast machine was an exemplar of what makes campaign finance laws so difficult to promulgate and implement, the use of public power to distribute economic goods (in the form of public works contracts) in return for campaign contributions and influence over economic decisions such as the awarding of jobs. Truman worked with the organization, but refused to grant contracts on any basis but economic costs and benefits and the law.

A story Truman enjoyed telling dealt with Pendergast's reaction to this situation. Five people met in Pendergast's office: Pendergast, Harry, and three contractors, all old friends of the organization and all extremely upset over Truman's refusal to award them contracts.

"These boys tell me that you won't give them contracts," Pendergast began.

"They can get them if they are low bidders, but they won't get paid for them unless they come up to specifications," answered Harry.

"Didn't I tell you boys," said Pendergast. "He's the contrariest cuss in Missouri."

The contractors left, and Pendergast told Harry to go ahead and run things as he thought best, adding only that of course he, Pendergast, always had the two other judges [the county officers who granted public works contracts] to call on if he needed to vote Harry down.

Did Truman understand, when he recounted the story, that it made clear where the real power lay? Or did he simply think that the votes Pendergast controlled (either the two judges or the electoral votes controlled by the machine) were qualitatively different from the votes Truman's stand attracted? Could Pendergast reply to Truman's telling of the story, to the implicit claim of an incompatibility between the politics he practiced and the principles of law and economic morality to which Truman adhered?

Pendergast could begin by defining politics in market terminology as the selling (if only to the powerholder) of the dream that we (the elected and those who vote) can control the future. Politics, in short, deals with emotional needs about which (because they change so quickly and for such a variety of reasons) we cannot be wholly transparent with ourselves or with each other; and the price determined by the political sale is the cost of change or lack of change, the balance we are willing to strike between means and ends, aspirations and techniques, needs and wants.

"You may, Harry, not like the political market, and I agree that attempts to regulate it will constantly be absorbed. But it does have a function. Money may be an arbitrary measuring rod that signifies nothing, but its use makes possible a comparison of incommensurables, and thus enables us to wage political struggles without a threat of imminent violence."

"If law contains the equitable possibility that the given instance may be an exception to the rule, moreover, then the question becomes, not whether we should obey the law, but what the law should be.

Admittedly, if that question is how the judge should decide the given case, we can do no more than ask that he or she do the best they can, but if we treat the issue as one of process, the question becomes how the law ought to be made compatible with your Utopian ideals, whether we can create a structure that expresses those ideals."

Democracy is in theoretical terms political capitalism, the rational will of the people (which includes its emotional expression) structuring a market in which votes, functioning like money, produce the political capital known as power. Do you agree? If not, why not? If so, why is this preferable to politically sophisticated authoritarianism?

CHAPTER 4:
LAW, POLITICS AND PRESIDENT CLINTON

Law and the Art of Politics

I

The human need for truth, for relevance rather than rationalization, creates the phenomenon known as art. It takes craft to create an objectivity that can withstand analysis, and craft is necessary to make a personal truth persuasive to others. Craft, however, is insufficient, because truth, propositions which persuade, is a question as much of relevance as of objective truth.

It is law that has been relevant for me, and my philosophy is produced by the transmogrification of United States law from a profession, a service industry like the clergy, into a business, in which, as with sports and entertainment figures and corporate executives, the question of value becomes what the market will bear in terms of monetary reward. Substantively, moreover, the passage of years has witnessed the erosion both of the precedent as a guide to decision and of federalism, the keystones of the structure I was taught. Both, to a considerable extent, are now perceived as technical arguments deployed against political correctness, as opposition to such correct results as *Brown v. Board of Education*. I believe my philosophy has come to terms with the implications of this situation. The question is whether I can confirm that belief by applying my philosophy persuasively to what I perceive as a parallel transformation in the nature of property.

The starting point is Charles Reich's famous article that defined government services as entitlements and hence as property. That this is not an idiosyncratic view is demonstrated by the fact that a case so holding in connection with welfare introduces many contemporary law students to the study of legal procedure. The contemporary connection between law and property, in short, is one product of the Legal Realist perspective on legal categories: property is what the judge says it is.

Unlike economic analysis, this perspective makes no claim about rationality. Property is the product of the rule of law rather than the market because it is not about rationality but about ownership, about the ability to do what you want with something. Insofar as property is private, moreover, property is about liberty, about not being restricted by social rules or conventions.

It is in this latter connection – the public/private dichotomy – that a tension arises between law and politics, between the legal rules that define the social institution of property and the culture that governs the way people behave, those habitual acts which, when they require justification, are designated political.

My thesis is that property, which was once a structural social element, is becoming accepted as the evolving product of a legal process, and that this shift is part of an ongoing cultural progression known as the bourgeois revolution, a shift from combat to the vote, from force to law as the paradigmatic political process, the latter being the way the culture is expressed.

Culture is the socio portion of a socioeconomic reality, the non-material element in a materialist view of reality. It is, in other words, what makes a given society unique, those things, for example, that make countries adopting democratic capitalist institutions imitations rather than reproductions of the United States, people adopting without necessarily accepting the cultural elements underlying the American way of doing things.

III

The United States dominates the world's economic marketplace because it consumes so large a proportion of the available resources. The American version of democratic capitalism had its origins in England, which (as Great Britain) dominated a world that was entering the industrial age because it had gotten there first, because it was the pioneer in working out the socioeconomic consequences of the bourgeois revolution.

In cultural political terms, the bourgeois revolution involved the replacement of the tribe by the nation, the social by the geo-political unit. An earlier shift from social to political had taken place in Rome, where the Senate, a collection of more-or-less equal barons who dealt with public matters by consensual action, was replaced by an Emperor wielding political power. After the collapse of that Empire, a feudal system developed in which property became a structural social element, the ownership of which involved acceptance of social and political responsibilities, an economic manifestation, so to speak, of the social and political reality of a tribe. In a tribe, every member sees the other members, including the tribal leaders, as variations of him or herself, which is what makes the phenomenon social as well as political. In feudal Europe, however, politics continued to be identified with the

Roman Empire and individuals participating in the political process represented a variety of tribes, all of whom, in one way or another – either as members, mercenaries or opponents – had been associated with the imperial political structure. Feudal property, in short, served the structural function it did precisely because it was "neutral," because, until it was reduced to private ownership, it lacked any identification with any given tribe or any given polity.

The monarchy – the family that eventually won the feudal competition for political power – substituted for the personal goal of the feudal lord the common goal that had characterized the political operations of the Roman Republic and, to a lesser extent, the Empire that succeeded it. One of the means employed by the monarchy to achieve this transition, to identify armed conflict as something employed in foreign as opposed to domestic affairs, was to assert and establish that its power derived, to some extent, from the authority wielded by the Church. To preserve that power, moreover, monarchs over time pre-empted the social and economic functions performed by the feudal barons, and thus gradually made illegitimate armed challenges to royal authority by these domestic rivals.

One of the most significant such transfers in England was that of law, the authority to resolve disputes, which increasingly involved obtaining writs, interpreted by the royal and ecclesiastical judiciary as defining causes of action, justifications for invoking royal authority. England, moreover, had been conquered by the Normans who assumed the monarchy. Consequently, property in England was the product of royal consent, thus making it logical to associate property with law, and to regard both as simultaneously involving subservience to monarchical authority, and a measure of freedom, a guarantee of order, from that authority.

IV

The next step, not only in England, but throughout Europe, was consciousness of, and the effort to rationalize, the incomplete transition from tribe to nation. Like all significant cultural events, the Enlightenment can best be understood by assessing it in functional individual human terms. The Enlightenment resulted in a revolutionary assault on established (monarchical) authority, something that, in individual human terms, happens when an adolescent believes that he or she understands what they are being taught, and is therefore prepared to challenge the existing order. Such a challenge is launched in the name of whatever cultural/political formulation is in fashion, or in opposition to that formulation as a disguised continuation of existing order.

The Enlightenment thinker most clearly described in these terms, a philosopher often cited as attacking rather than representing the Enlightenment, is Rousseau. Rousseau grasped the concept of the nation-state, the legal entity that had replaced the tribe and the Empire as the political manifestation of the culture. Rousseau created the nationstate, however, by postulating the impossible, a cultural homogeneity that could not exist in a community larger than a Greek polis. Philosophically, the Enlightenment was too sophisticated to be either Platonic, in the sense of searching for the essence of political truth, or Aristotelian, seeking simply to master the craft of finding political truth. Instead, it accepted the potentially contradictory political goals of liberty and equality, and reconciled them by promoting, in the guise of the tribal cultural virtue of fraternity, what the 19th century came to know as nationalism.

In the absence of the homogeneity postulated by Rousseau, the General Will, which gives legitimacy to political action, becomes the will either of the absolute democratic majority or of the politically sophisticated minority. The Enlightenment's solutions to this problem of how a nation can properly be governed – tolerant attitudes and scientific inquiry – are with us still. Because tolerant attitudes are, at least in theory, not the same as indifference, and because science and religion are, at least in theory, not competitive cultural ways of imposing order on the universe, the Enlightenment postulated that economic and social progress and rationality are synonymous, that the right thing to do – ethics for the individual, policy for the collective – can be arrived at by thought freed both from the emotional need for faith and from that personal inability to control one's emotions which leads one to rationalize one's acts rather than to seek the truth of what one is doing.

In the event, however, the Enlightenment did nothing more nor less than to secularize revolutionary aspirations. Saving humankind no longer meant reforming that Church which taught how life ought to be lived, the proper goal of human existence. Instead, the Enlightenment recognized that the Protestant Reformation had made the meaning of Scripture a personal matter, had made all individuals priests.

Being a priest is, of course, a significant responsibility. In political terms, it means that you hold an office, play a public role which predisposes other people to expect you to abide by higher standards than you would follow in your private conduct. It means, in short, that a republic can be a democracy, that the average person can take his or her place in the Senate.

When the fact that individuals are priests is forgotten, when the Senate defends a sinful departure from proper behavior because it has become part of the culture, the consequence, sooner or later, is revolution or, to be concrete, the New Deal of *Brown v. Board of Education*. It is, however, precisely the distinction between a republic and a democracy that, in the latter, public and private morality are permitted to coalesce as political power is used against aristocrats, thereby eroding the cultural power afforded those professing the observance of aristocratic codes of behavior.

The contradictions inherent in this unintended consequence of bourgeois progress are most clear in connection with armed conflict, what it is the individual is prepared to die for. In feudal times, the answer was the personal goals of the feudal lord. The bourgeois revolution substitutes the abstraction of the community for the concrete person of the feudal lord, and the Thirty Years War in Europe marked the transition from religious to national goals. It remains true, however, that the President is not only commander in chief, but, as such, has the power to initiate armed conflict even in the absence of a declaration of war by the Congress. We are in theory prepared to die, in other words, when the President decides that we should be.

The President envisioned by the Founders was a monarch without absolute powers (or powers other than executive powers), something our Constitution attempted to create by imposing restraints – checks and balances – on the monarchical power with which the Founders were familiar. It has taken more than two centuries for the contradictions implicit in this scheme to take center stage, embodied in the institution of an independent prosecutor who has available unlimited resources to force courts to resolve the political issues raised by technical questions of law concerning the scope of that authority. The unresolved question, therefore, is the nature of the executive power at this point in the transition known as the bourgeois revolution.

V

In the bourgeois world, the elected leader, the political reality for which our votes (or lack of votes) make us responsible, attempts to be, not some combination of the person the leader knows him or herself to be and the "public" person with whom the electorate interacts (either physically or through the media), but the "public" personality alone. It is this focus, this denial of part of the truth, which post-New Deal United States Presidents attribute to Franklin Roosevelt, in part no doubt because he so significantly increased the power both of the federal government and the Presidency.

Roosevelt, however, was an aristocrat, for whom the distinction between the social and the personal was a price one paid for having been born to privilege rather than a price to be paid for political power, for having been born with the responsibility to lead rather than having to be successful in persuading others to follow one's lead. Nonaristocratic presidents lack the serenity this aristocratic certainty gives one, and are thus in theory subject to that wearing introspection needed to determine whether a given use of presidential power is personal or legitimate, whether limits on that power are being exceeded. President Clinton, by requiring a series of rulings on questions of evidentiary privilege, forced federal courts to determine whether, and under what circumstances, this question can be answered for, as opposed to by, the president.

My thesis is that *Brown v. Board of Education*, because it was simultaneously judicial and political, is a precedent for that blurring of the boundaries between law and politics that characterized both the charges of scandal leveled against Clinton and the White House's response to them. It is clear that money provided by Clinton's political opponents financed much of the investigation that permits the charges to be made; but does that mean that those charges have no place in court? Similarly, it is clear that the charges themselves are often insufficient to state a legally cognizable cause of action; but if what makes them suspect is their political nature, why are the legal defects that prevent them from being heard in court dispositive of their validity? Finally, if the charges are based on a blurring of the lines between law and politics, why should Clinton eschew that blurring in defending himself?

The question, in other words, can be reduced to the definition of *Realpolitik*, what political realism amounts to. Thus, Clinton's fundamental argument is to conflate law and politics and to argue, in connection with whatever the specific event or issue is, that, as to law, he believes in doing the right thing and is in technical compliance with the law and that, as to politics, again, he believes in doing the right thing, and his concern is with the goal to be achieved rather than the ideology invoked to justify pursuit of the goal, the concrete result rather than the principle.

Analyzed purely in terms of its rhetoric, this argument rests on precisely the distinction between law and politics that was destroyed in theory by the Legal Realists and in practice by *Brown v. Board of Education*. Thus, law, unlike politics, is neutral, and technical compliance is all that can reasonably be asked. Politics, however, like all art, is a matter of the heart rather than the head, focusing on the goal to be achieved rather than the ideology used to justify pursuit of that goal.

Insofar as Clinton is willing to create the conditions that permit him to retain power, he is creating a given political situation, and that act of creation is the art of politics. The process of *Realpolitik* implies a setting of priorities or weighing of ends and means. In assessing the practitioners of *Realpolitik*, however, one cannot distinguish the art of political judgment from the craft of political calculation. How, then, does one judge a calculation which is simultaneously a work of art?

Art differs from craft, not because craft is not creative, but because art is accepted as being so. In the end, in other words, bourgeois art is a matter of appearance, of what it is perceived to be. Such an analysis is not applicable to classical art, which is directly expressive of a culture, and thus indistinguishable from craft.

The distinction occurs when art becomes mannerist, self-conscious about the effects that can be created. The authority of classical (Renaissance) art was recaptured (after a mannerist phase) during the period known as the baroque, and this artistic phenomenon was the product of the Counter-Reformation, the period when the Catholic Church began to compete for support, not as the institution looked to define human goals, but an abstraction that represented one's allegiance to non-material truth. What gave baroque art authority was not loyalty to an institution competing for the artist's services. The challenge was not to overcome the limitations of mannerism, nor to surrender one's awareness of the possibility of manipulating the truth, nor to overcome secular doubts. One's artistic style reflected, rather, the sincerity of one's desire to create art.

For Clinton, *Realpolitik* is a process that assumes rather than seeks proper motivation, not a willingness to sacrifice power to achieve the proper result, but a determination to use all necessary means to retain the political power necessary to continue the process of seeking the proper laws. Clinton, in short, is realistic about law, about applied politics, but cynically treats power as something other than a means, as something more significant than the ends for which it is used. This does not mean that his motivation to do the right thing is not sincere; it means only that Clinton is being realistic about the value of that motivation, about what must be sacrificed to remain in power.

In legal terms, Clinton's proponents assert that one must keep completely distinct political judgments about the work of President Clinton and moral judgments about the character of citizen William

Jefferson Clinton. There are those, however, for whom separation of church and state is a matter of functional rather than abstract principles, an attempt to free politics from coercive influence rather than an absolute commandment. For such persons, the question raised by President Clinton's conduct is whether his version of *Realpolitik* is necessary, the precise nature of capitalist democratic politics and law.

The Science of Politics

The attempt in this course has been to lay the groundwork for a science of politics, a *Realpolitik* without cynicism. Thus: aspirational emotions create potentially good politics. In philosophical terms, they are Platonic Forms, attempts to achieve classic art, to implement one's (personal or social) culture, a state simultaneously ethical and epistemological, being what one should be. This interpretation of *The Republic* makes it relevant by viewing politics as an Aristotlean process, a modification that enables one to create a model of the process. Politicians are defined by this model as social artists, persons who impose a pattern on socioeconomic experience, either by science – glorifying the political procedures defined by the existing culture – religion – projecting the need for such glorification onto a mysterious force – or art, finding the pattern implicit in the chaotic set of individual feelings that, at any given moment, constitutes the single frame that one can derive from the ongoing motion picture known as culture.

Emotions, the quanta of this science of politics, are the fundamental cultural unit: either abstract justifications for forces or feelings, or the consequence of one's production of, or interaction with, forces or feelings. Feelings are the consequences of sensory data or abstractions from that data, and, in the case of abstractions from sensory data, the feeling has itself become the emotion.

The theoretical deficiencies from which the science of economics suffers are its definition of process as something rational rather than emotional and its choice of the individual rather than the institution as the unit whose behavior is being described. My science, if it is accepted as valid, postulates emotion as the fundamental unit and connects the individual and institutions in terms of that unit, by defining culture as the social manifestation of the contemporary set of individual emotions. Politics, in terms of this science, can be modeled as a process governed by inertia and momentum, and issues raised by the nature of momentum – the sense in which politics can be said to be path dependent – are questions the Chartist need not ask and answers that the Fundamentalist takes on faith: whether force needs a cause, whether reality is more than a process, whether, in short, politics (anymore than theology or law or economics) can answer the important questions.

These queries can be accepted as unanswerable, because the investigation we are conducting is scientific as well as spiritual, because a force, once reduced to a quantum, is to that extent tamed. Statistics are the consequence of this taming, however, and statistics function as a limit, rather than an input, in terms of the model. The problem being investigated, therefore, is how to make social science relevant: the basis from which to deduce a jurisprudential framework for capitalist democracy and the Utopian Constitution to which we should all aspire.

I do so by defining culture as social friction, the political element that was discarded as economics became mathematical rather than behavioral. Given this definition, social matter – the institutions that frame social reality – is a balance of force and friction, whereas social energy – the process that shapes those institutions – is the product of force and friction. Force is needed to overcome internal friction, the resistance to change known as inertia. Inertia is a state produced both by formal truth – by the extent to which clear communication is arbitrary because it fails adequately to describe the chaotic sensory data and feelings by means of which we connect with "out there," – and by corruption, the desire of those in power not to adapt, to keep things as they are, to remain in power.

The political problem, therefore, is that of balancing force and culture, and dealing with that problem involves dealing with components of motivation: love, the play of power and *hubris*, the sin of pride. A concrete example of an attempt to deal with these issues is the unsuccessful impeachment of President William Jefferson Clinton, the next issue this course will consider.

Judging the Politics of Capitalist Democracy
CXXIX

> The expense of spirit in a waste of shame
> Is lust in action; and till action, lust
> Is perjured, murderous, bloody, full of blame,
> Savage, extreme, rude, cruel, not to trust;
> Enjoy'd no sooner but despised straight;
> Past reason hunted; and no sooner had,
> Past reason hated, as a swallowed bait,
> On purpose laid to make the taker mad:
> Mad in pursuit, and in possession so;
> Had, having, and in quest to have, extreme;
> A bliss in proof, and proved, a very woe;
> Before, a joy proposed; behind, a dream.
>   All this the world well knows; yet none knows well
>   To shun the heaven that leads men to this hell

Q. I'll accept your political science, but what is this nonsense about "the play of power?" The question is whether what happened was a crime.

Perhaps the problem is that you confuse the resolution of disputes which characterizes common law with criminal proceedings. Thus, common law is about deriving rules from wrestling with their applications; criminal law is about defining wrongs by struggling to do something about them. My position is that what Clinton did was lust rather than love, therefore a sin, and that he should have been impeached for doing it.

A. First of all, the legal issue is perjury, not sin. Second, the question of good law (and equity is part of good law) is the applicability of your category, and your characterization of Clinton's act is the category so accurately described in the Shakespearean sonnet.

Clinton agrees that what he was doing involved a wrong, but claims that what happened was a relationship rather than "lust in action." Admittedly, that claim could be a lie, but accepting a lie as truth is the risk entailed in judging human activity, in deciding what the law should be. The problem, in my view, is that what Clinton calls relationship is, for him, the emotional certainty that a relationship can be purely pleasurable, the mannerist faith that if one says (and/or believes) that the other is precisely what one wants, intention and reality will become indistinguishable.

This blurring of the line between love and power, truth and emotion, self and others, is culturally glorified as the catalyst that transforms the sexual drive into the creation of a family. A family, however, like a church, is a political and, when functional, spiritual (but not necessarily a romantic) relationship. In the end, in other words, Clinton's romances, like his politics, are mannerist exercises which make it impossible to determine whether what is happening is being produced by feeling or manipulation. Even when it is mannerist, however, I cannot find art to be an unforgivable sin.

Q. I don't deny that you have a right to your opinion, but why should I accept it? Equity means that when, as in the case of Martin Luther King, Jr., the power you exercise is spiritual, you may be guilty of sin but non-culpable. The question, however, is why I am wrong in believing that emotions such as lust are evil.

A. Sin is evil, and, like any human system, equity can be perceived as arbitrary. Distinguishing King from Clinton is, therefore, a hard case, and faith alone does not resolve a hard case.

My thesis is that a good life is about pursuit of the Form of faith, attempting to make politics, conscious behavior, true to faith. Persons who are religious may be content in a way denied to those who are cynics, but, unlike those who are spiritual, people subject to a theology, rather than those, like King, who live it, are not aware that they have a choice, that faith can be a personal decision as well as a social context. Consequently, it's not that I wouldn't vote to convict someone who feels his sympathetic nature entitles him to deny sinful acts; it's simply that what I think is important is humility, the constant awareness that one may be wrong.

Q. I find that wonderful rhetoric, but I'm a simple lawyer, so I'm not sure I agree. Sex is sex and love is love and you have the burden, if love is the play of power, of demonstrating how the twain shall meet.

A. No I don't. Sexual love is an act, what is happening at the moment; marriage is a state, the attempt to convert the act into structure, into something impervious to time; and eros – human love – is the feeling, the remembrance or habit that, in theory, marks the transformation of one into the other.

That transformation is sacramental, not because the church requires marriage, but because marriage, like the church, is Utopian, an attempt to accept while transforming the here and now. The sacramental nature of love is, as a result, a spiritual or artistic fact as opposed to a religious truth; and the art inherent in Shakespeare's sonnet is that it assumes the connection between act and state embodied in love, and denominates as lust the absence of the transformation. The sonnet makes clear that political culture – letting Clinton go unpunished –can be perceived as a restraint, as limiting what is right.

Q. So liberty, being free to seek the true path, is escape from restraint?

A. Partially, but it's also a danger. Power corrupts, and liberty – the substitute for faith embodied in the Bill of Rights – can all too easily become (like religion) the rationalization for evading those givens embodied in the cultural movie citizens of a democratic capitalist society are all producing.

Q. So a good government is an Oscar winning motion picture, a culture made conscious?

A. I'm afraid you can perceive this capitalist democracy that way, and certainly Clinton sees the world much as the people in Dreamworks would portray it, but I'm not sure you understand what this attempt at dialog has been about. I'm trying to educate you about the nature of faith, the need for humility, not change the time frame that determines your emotional self, something only you can do.

Your question is the question politics is about, what an accurate description of today's reality means in terms of action, of what tomorrow should be; whether one wants to embark on dialog, whether one's spirituality (or lack thereof), while true for oneself, can be put aside sufficiently to make it possible to entertain other people's truths. Humility without faith is the end without the means, and can therefore be characterized as a more pure Form, but my lesson is not an attempt to define the nature of the Form. It is, rather, a justification for pursuing it, obeying the philosopher-king who is the person one should be.

The remaining question, therefore, is the nature of today's philosopher king, the choice between Hand's spirituality and Holmes' cynicism.

Q. You may be right about politics, but what does that have to do with law? Our argument, after all, is ultimately about abuse of power and the Constitution. Thus, your position seems to be that Clinton abused his power as President, that the Senate abused its power by not voting for impeachment, and that judges are abusing their power to interpret the Constitution. If a democratic capitalist Constitution does not grant powers, however, what is its function? And once those powers are granted, the possibility of abuse necessarily exists.

A. I agree that you are raising the relevant questions, but I note that those questions are inherent in the concept of the philosopher king. Thus Socrates, whose ideas Plato thought he was communicating, would have opposed *The Republic* as a guide to action because it was written rather than oral, and, as such, like the art he feared, embodied an objectivity, a concreteness, incompatible with the universal applicability of the Form.

Given this philosophical starting point, it is clear that the objection to Cardozo is that he is an artist, producing a truth whose certainty stems from the clarity of a private vision rather than being a concrete decision that becomes part of the judicial culture. The issue you raise, therefore, is whether Hand's position is tenable, whether, given the choice, Holmes is the only realistic possibility.

Should you deny certiorari in the following case? Why or why not?

Both the district court and the court of appeals have refused to overturn denial of conscientious objector status (the United States having reinstituted the draft) on the basis that, because the person claiming the status described her or himself as an atheist with spiritual objections to war, the board that refused the status was correct in holding that any decision would be wholly arbitrary, and that, in such a situation, the community which had declared a state of war to be in existence had rights greater than those of the individual because it consisted of more than the complaining individual.

CHAPTER 5:
THE PLATONIC FORM OF UNITED STATES LAW

The Philosopher King and Judging

Shakespeare was describing the Renaissance, a world in which ethics and epistemology began to separate and economic activity became something produced by political as well as cultural mandates. Shakespeare speaks for us all because the Renaissance began an historical process, a process which made being spiritual committing to the possibility of non-material truth rather than governing one's actions by precepts derived from the obligation (to oneself and one's Higher Power) to lead a good life. That process made it possible wholeheartedly to accept the machine, to subordinate other humans to the rule of steam and iron and oneself to the mandate of the clock.

Shakespeare was describing the Western world as it was between the Protestant Reformation and the Enlightenment, a society characterized by religious civil wars, and Hobbes was the philosopher who offered a solution. The Leviathan state Hobbes prescribed exercised arbitrary power, but Hobbes' focus was not on the state but rather on the problem of creating a religious body, a church which would serve a meaningful function in everyday life. The Founding Fathers dealt with the problem of church and state by incorporating in the Bill of Rights contradictory provisions about religion, a prohibition on establishment combined with a guarantee of free exercise. The First Amendment also contains a mandate about speech, which the Warren

Court interpreted as completely separating expression from action, an oversimplification of social interaction produced by the romantic view of community as liberty, a world in which institutional religious truth is indistinguishable from private spiritual or emotional belief, a secular ideology in which neither dogma nor heresy exist.

How far this process of transforming political power from sacred leadership into secular rights – the bourgeois revolution – has progressed is the question how far the processes known as life are regarded as subject to human control as opposed to being treated as mysteries beyond human comprehension. It is in their answers to this question that Hand, Holmes and Cardozo differ.

Thus, Cardozo is untroubled by the question of the legitimacy of the power he is exercising in making law and Holmes thinks all power ultimately illegitimate. In lectures he gave on the Bill of Rights, Hand justified restraint on judicial activity by asking whether we wished to be ruled by Platonic Guardians. He made an exception for the First Amendment, presumably because he regarded freedom of speech and/or separation of church and state as essential to American culture.

Hand's plea is for restraint of the *hubris* inherent in the certainty that one is righting an injustice, the judicial willingness to acquiesce in an entitlement to defy the culture that gives one the constitutional right to do so. Such restraint, however, recognition of the difference between individual liberty and the fraternal feeling of freedom produced by equality, is incompatible with the First Amendment. For Plato, moreover, Guardians represented, not philosopher kings, but the politics practiced in Sparta, a society dedicated to the winning of wars. Hand's question to the philosopher king, therefore, is what the American Constitution without a Bill of Rights would be. The answer is Utopian.

Constitution of the State of Utopia

1. Utopians recognize that law is no more and no less than the supremely necessary social myth. Utopians subscribe to the reality of law by having created this Constitution.

2. Utopian government consists of three branches. The executive enforces the law. The legislature decrees rules and interprets them. The judiciary finds facts whenever such facts determine the law's applicability.

3. (i) Any statutory term so specifically defined that no discretion is possible in its application is a rule. All other statutory terms are matters of fact.

(ii) Any enforcement action must be accompanied by a statement designating the legislative rules on which it is based. Interpretations by the executive of rules, whether procedural or substantive, are subject to veto by vote of the legislature. Applications of rules by the executive are subject to interpretation in a later judicial proceeding.

4. The three bodies of law in this state subject to the Constitution are:

A. <u>Representation</u>

(i) Any constituency which desires representation within the legislature may contract with the legislature for such representation. The resultant contract is subject to this Constitution.

(ii) All government officials must either be elected or appointed, and elected officials serve until replaced by a referendum held by the electing constituency. Property owned by persons elected to office must be surrendered to the state, and elected officials may receive no income other than their government stipend or pension whether or not still serving in office. Other officials can be appointed, but only by elected officials still serving in office.

(iii) So long as the representative who took office as the result of an election in which he or she participated continues to serve in a legislative capacity, Utopians cannot participate in a second election involving legislative office, unless they affiliate with a constituency not represented in the legislature within the prior fifty years.

(iv) Any entity engaged in economic activities in Utopia whose capitalization or income equals or exceeds the assets of any of the constituencies represented in the legislature must pay that excess amount as a dividend, when it is received or accrued, whichever would occur first.

B. Crime

(i) Public crimes involve violence against persons or risk of physical injury to persons and must be proven to a reasonable certainty. The death penalty is permissible.

(ii) Private crimes must be proven by a preponderance of the evidence. Treble damages are permissible. Private crimes, however, until proven, may not be halted if a bond has been posted equal in amount to the injury alleged.

C. Taxation

(i) The Utopian government may obtain funds solely by issuing bonds or by assessment of an asset tax applicable to all property of whatever kind, with the exception of certificates of ownership in those economic governments known as corporations, in connection with which gain (even if potential) must be realized before the certificate can be treated as an economic as opposed to political asset. The asset tax, payable yearly by all Utopians, applies to any assets greater than ten times the median Utopian income, and to other assets at rates to be decreed by the legislature. Only amounts spent on capital improvements can be funded by the issuance of bonds, but no portion of the police budget may be treated as capital in nature.

(ii) For purposes of this Constitution military activities are police matters dealing with foreign affairs, and all such matters are subject to the rules of any international organization to which Utopia subscribes. Such a subscription is to be treated as constitutional rather than contractual in nature.

A Philosophy of Law

Q. What sort of Constitution is this? The government it creates is so tied in knots that it obviously won't be able to work.

A. The government created by the Utopian Constitution is a government of law and whether such a government can work is a matter of faith. The first Article is Utopian recognition of that fact.

Q. No it isn't. The first Article doesn't say law is a matter of faith; it says law is a social myth, and what social myth means to me is the collective rationalization of individual behavior that is habitual rather than consciously rational.

A. You're correct if we are speaking in the context of psychology or sociology. In philosophical terms, however, we could also call the Constitution a Platonic Form. Aristotle was correct, of course, in noting the abstract nature of the Platonic Form, but Aristotle's own obsessive focus on the concrete nature of reality ignored the need for context as the necessary framework in terms of which the specific instance is interpreted and given meaning. The question, therefore, is not whether the Constitution is real, but the nature of the reality it is intended to embody. Thus, Utopians do not ask how one gets there from here, but rather focus on where one wants to go.

Q. Well, what about that? What sort of society is Utopia? Liberal? Conservative? Capitalist? Socialist?

A. Let's untangle the political, social and economic knot your four terms present. The issue is the individual and others, whether those others are political, economic or social actors. The more the individual incorporates — a significant other, legitimated children, identification with a group — the more the individual identifies him or her self as a social actor. The question raised by your four categories, therefore, is how Utopian society manifests itself politically and economically in the context of its relationship with the given individual.

In this context, I see liberal and conservative as terms describing forms of political leadership. Liberal leaders know what those who are governed need; conservative leaders know why what the governed have is worth preserving. Capitalism and socialism, on the other hand, are descriptions of alternative ways of structuring power.

Capitalism describes a society in which economic and political bureaucracy — the locus of institutionalized power — is decentralized. Most manifestations of socialism are distinguishable from capitalism only because their bureaucracies are eventually centralized. The theory of socialism, however, is that it is different from capitalism in that its operations are political rather than economic, the expression of the shared value rather than the market.

In this sense, Utopia is socialist, and most capitalist countries (certainly all governments ruling capitalist countries) subscribe to social theory. The proof of this in the case of Utopia is the death penalty provision. It's difficult to operate on shared values if you're not willing to enforce them. There is, of course, the alternative of imprisonment, but unless the country is remarkably repressive in a social sense, there will be a considerable number of public crimes, and it is unlikely that a rational society not repressing the desires of its individual members would be willing to pay the costs involved in making long-term imprisonment preferable to death.

Q. I think I understand the Utopian criminal system. The structure of the government means it's difficult to convict anyone and the current nature of the police budget maximizes the attention individual members of the society will give to police activity. Maybe that's the best humans can do in dealing with power. But the last provision in the Constitution makes participation in international police activities constitutional rather than contractual. As I understand it, that means Utopian constitutional safeguards may not be applicable.

A. I'm glad to see that, wherever you went to school, they trained you as a sophisticated constitutional lawyer. You're right of course. Let's take a concrete example. Assume a rational world in which the possibility of nuclear holocaust is solved by disarmament. Enforcement of such an arrangement would require existence of an international authority with at least potential access to nuclear weapons, and constitutional guarantees simply could not be enforced against such an authority, even if it were rational to do so. That, of course, is the nature of power – and the Utopian Constitution deals with power.

Q. Well, then, why disarm? Indeed, why be rational?

A. Because material power is not all there is; there is also spiritual love, agape rather than eros, loving the power that creates things as they are rather than the art that embodies things as we feel they should be. That distinction, though theoretical, is culturally enforced as the taboo against incest. It is the distinction between the tenderness a parent feels for a child and the tenderness a lover feels for the object of his or her love.

Q. I trust you can tell me the practical difference. How do I know which one is appropriate in any given context?

A. As to the two types of love, the distinction is between the freedom to be loving and the power liberty gives one to do what one wants. As to love and power, the answer is determined by how one perceives the situation in which the question arises. One looks for power when one needs it; one gives love when one has it. The balance between eros and agape determines the philosopher king one should be, and the Utopian hope is that that balance can be made operational in the world, that faith in oneself can be maintained.

Q. Now I'm beginning to understand the Utopian constitution. But what of the problem of church and state, the possibility that we are indeed a Christian nation?

A. Christ's sacrifice is love. Jesus was Jewish, but the Crucifixion is a universal gift rather than the sacred symbol of a tribe. Not that the universal nature of the gift comes without cost, since the monotheism that was the contribution of the tribe to human progress is now burdened with the ambiguity and complexity of the Trinity.

Ambiguity and complexity, on the other hand, are what life is about. Religion, after all, is the antithesis of spirituality, which is only real when it is individual as opposed to social reality. The nature of love, therefore, depends on who you are, and the political question is whether there is a place for it in our world.

Q. What of Hand's opposing *Brown* because it could not be justified by precedents? Was *that* being loving?

A. One possible response is that Hand was wrong because what Adam Smith called sympathy – mercy and compassion rather than humility – is always appropriate. Such a response, however, raises the question of the extent to which humans are social animals. Insofar as they are, their actions are determined by their culture, the series of necessary albeit arbitrary discriminations that distinguishes their from other societies. The issue raised by disapproval of *Brown* is, therefore, when it is proper to impose your view on those subject to the power you exercise, why you should attempt to use the law to change other people's culture.

To behave validly – to be certain that one has been purged of the sin of pride – is not to be right, but constantly to be aware of the possibility of being wrong, to accept as crucially important the fact that how one attains truth or justice is not a matter of calculable certainty. Moral claims, as litigators demonstrate every day, are tactical counters in the competitive – because uncertain – search for truth and justice. Spiritual truth acknowledges that things are not all calculable, that spiritual love is real and yet mysterious, and therefore expressed as forces and entities worshiped in various ways by the societies in terms of which individual humans define themselves.

The claim of moral authority which underlies your question is a claim of moral power. It may not be a material claim, but it is an assertion of power nonetheless, and, as such, it predisposes one to ignore the possibility that one's moral goal may conflict with other, equally desirable aims, or involve short-term harms that outweigh the possible long-run advantages. The *Brown* opinion itself refused explicitly to overrule *Plessy v. Ferguson*, which had adopted separate-but-equal as the legal standard, no doubt because such a ruling would have underlined the extent to which it was the existing law that was the problem. Whether the opinion in *Brown* was something one should have joined, whether the court should simply have gone on deciding, case by case, that no separate system was in fact equal, is a personal question that can only be resolved by and for oneself. A judge can be said to have erred when a higher court reverses the result or if the reasoning in the opinion is demonstrably illogical. In other cases, on issues we designate matters of judgment, one can say only that one disagrees, that one is saddened that the truth that law is not identical with justice has blinded the judge with whom one disagrees to the fact that, to the extent justice can officially be done in the United States, its social embodiment is the law.

Governing by law rather than bureaucracy carries with it the possibility that authority can be equitable, that the implementation of the Constitutional or legislative rule will be governed as much by the question of justice – the craft involved in applying a rule to a particular situation – as by the exigencies of power, the need to make the rule credible by applying it across the board. It is in connection with the craft of equity – the decision whether the plea that the rule not be applied is a request for an exception or an attempt at evasion – that the distinction between personal and legal authority becomes a matter of perception, the truth being either that a rule is being tailored to the circumstances or that the law is being ignored, something explicable by self-interest, corruption, or an attempt to please a constituency not making an appearance in the case being decided. Once equity ceases to be an ecclesiastical mystery, in other words, it becomes like law, a matter of applied politics, of power rather than justice, a situation in which equity becomes, in system terms a matter of odds and in personal terms a matter of luck or chance. Faith in precedent, in the system of law, is a rational response by a judge to this situation.

Q. Utopia seems to me to include the worst aspects of the country we live in, the death penalty at home and acceptance of war as inevitable in foreign affairs. Why are these necessary; and why do you insist on characterizing them as Utopian?

A. The short answer is that culture, even when Utopian, is what one is faced with, not the environment as one would like it to be.

Q. Your short answer ignores the fact that one's political philosophy defines what one does, the balance one strikes between ends and means. Perhaps the problem is your admiration for Hand's rational faith, something you admit constrained him in that it denied him access to the art manifested in the opinions of Holmes and Cardozo.

A. I admire Hand because, unlike Holmes and Cardozo, he attempts not to impose his philosophy on others. He is aware, in other words, of the constraint involved in the possibility of mannerism, the fact that, once baroque art is impossible, once spirituality replaces religion, the choice is not between romanticism and classicism, but between humility and manipulation.

Q. But how is humility and/or spirituality compatible with the death penalty?

A. Socrates imposed the death penalty on himself, and the Platonic Form my philosophy espouses is a matter of process as much as substance. It is Utopian only in the sense that it acknowledges the requirement of faith, that one cannot be certain of reaching the right result. The content of that faith is the attempt to achieve serenity, to accept reality by refusing to succumb to the romantic preference for attempting to change the world rather than examining one's motivation.

Q. Art is not synonymous with reality, and an impressive rhetorical argument is, therefore, not necessarily a valid one. What impresses me is that most developed countries have both abolished the death penalty and supported instruments of international law like the International Criminal Court we refuse to join. Does Utopia propose to abolish evolution?

A. The problem with evolution is not that of rational science as opposed to emotional art, but that, like most effective theory, it encourages a confusion of ends and means. Individuals interact with, and are therefore changed by as well as changing the environment, but those who survive are fittest only for the end of survival, and the mutations that create those changes are creating an order which may or may not be lawful, a pattern which may or may not be what an artist would denominate design. Evolution is real, in other words, even in Utopia, but the cause and effect the scientist is postulating remains an imposition on a possibly chaotic reality, an aesthetic preference for order, an insistence that things make sense, that spirituality, because mysterious, is unnecessary.

Finally, as to the use of law to regulate war, I agree that engaging in war is an irrational act, but its declaration by properly constituted authority may be produced by a valid perception of a need for change, for the sort of "creative destruction" a capitalist economic system imposes on social and economic institutions. The issue, as in all political matters that one attempts to transform into issues of law, is the choice between applying a consensus or attempting to reach the right result in the particular concrete instance, pragmatic judgment or an ideology which encourages extrapolation as well as experiment, assuming order rather than complexity and harmony rather than disagreement and anticipated reactions.

Q. I'll grant that science is no better than art in distinguishing substantive from instrumental tools, a distinction necessary to the choice between ends and means, and it is help with that choice, I agree, that makes law a profession. The question, however, is why the concept of rights is not the proper means for accomplishing this task. Excesses can occur, of course, but perfection is an aspiration rather than a goal, and you have the burden of proving the argument that individual rights are the problem rather than the solution.

A. My argument is not that rights are the problem, but that constitutional rights as interpreted by the Warren Court – legal as opposed to cultural privileges and immunities – are symptoms of the damage done to the structure of United States government and society by the New Deal's replacement of federalism with bureaucratic expertise. Population growth and global interdependence may have made the process inevitable, but the fact remains that bureaucracy is both rationalized culture internally and an attempt to rationalize the society on which it is imposed.

Thus, once economic and political rights are declared, they produce institutions (both governmental and non-governmental) dedicated to expanding them. The individual's search for freedom from bureaucracy, therefore, is today a matter of relying on the system of checks and balances, the division of powers that constitutes the art of successful republican government, that creates three political groups with goals and methods that may or may not be compatible, each convinced that its interpretation of the powers granted it by the Constitution is correct.

The system of checks and balances, however, was the product of a culture which knew that power corrupted, which trusted a Higher Power – an abstraction rather than the Entity that justified religious power – to oversee the operations of a system designed to stalemate power, and which did not confuse that Higher Power with such non-personal abstractions as the public, the voter, or the reasonable man or woman cited by law professors. The danger today is that the legislature, executive and judiciary have been freed from the culture that created checks and balances, and are therefore engaged in a corrupt competition for political leadership, a race to use the rule of law to transform rights from the ability to resist government power into entitlements to wealth and immunity from the consequences of the tragic human condition – the likelihood of *hubris* – that makes checks and balances necessary.

Q. As I understand your philosophy now, Utopia is an attempt to make enlightenment aspirations realistic. Perhaps you are correct philosophically, but the issue for me remains that of the connection, if any, between that attempt and the practice of law.

A. Law is a cultural manifestation; and good law is therefore the product of an observer as much as a participant, someone in control of her or his emotions, applying rather than imposing a political philosophy, dealing with rather than expressing what one feels. The choice for the judge is that between following the law or making it. The practicing lawyer, who interprets the law, has the choice between reading what the judge did as an instrument of policy or an attempt to do equity, and that choice involves the question whether the decision is imposing the judge's style or acknowledging the claims of history, of the *status quo*, of precedent and equilibrium.

From the client's point of view, in short, both the judge and the lawyer bear responsibility for the law, and the problem for the judge and/or lawyer is to make the connection between emotions and behavior, to understand the forces that produce the choice one makes. An infant, we have postulated, becomes political by obtaining pleasing results from action or speech. That result, in some instances, is perceived as associated with context, with the material environment. When the result is not pleasing, we have the first basis for culture, the story that transforms the physical fact of feeling into the basis for speech or action known as information. Confronted with pain, one's story creates categories, personal stereotypes, which account for one's own or the environment's behavior, and the art created by these stories constitutes the set of interlocking metaphors rather than formulas that permit people to coexist in relationships more abstract than tribal ones, to accept differences as well as similarities, creating complex emotional situations to which scientific formulas cannot effectively be applied.

The next stage is awareness of the distinction between the private and public self, between who one is and the self that interacts with others, whose actions define the choice between competition and cooperation. This stage produces the distinction between reality and rationality, the facts of politics – feelings and emotions – and the market that produces goods and services which serve as incentives for participating in, and rewards for mastering, market processes, and which, in sufficient quantities or as the result of historical associations, constitute luxury, the promise of escape from those processes, an escape embodied in the cultural products recognized as art.

The final stage that precedes and produces adult behavior is adolescence, how one responds to the existence of sexual desire, whether the resultant emotions and actions produce sympathy for an individual or response to a stereotype produced by the prior stories. Adult behavior is conscious of the distinction between a stereotype and the sympathy underlying the Golden Rule. It is that sympathy which is embodied in agape, and the common law is human recognition of the fact that equality – the basis for humility – can all too easily become a rationalization for attempting to make the world – as opposed to oneself – what it ought to be. A Cardozo opinion, for example, often does justice at the cost of distorting the facts of the dispute it is adjudicating. Similarly, the liberty to become the person one ought to be can all too easily become a rationalization for accepting injustice.

Q. This is the second time you've defined justice. I thought you saw justice as purely personal. Was I wrong?

A. No. Justice, like all ends (and justice is an end sought by means of law) is the product of the story one tells oneself to relieve pain, the image of the possibility of happiness. The modern version of that story is to transform freedom – negative rights – into liberty, the positive version of happiness.

Q. What's wrong with seeking happiness?

A. The confusion of that story with truth. Positive and negative are process terms, energy functioning as attraction or repulsion; liberty and freedom are perceptions of the environment which account for emotions, substantive as well as instrumental ends produced by political art, escapes from the audiences defined by the stories we have told ourselves.

Modern theory attempts to cope with the relativity of our environment, the fact that the rate at which time passes for oneself is either a formal convention or variable substantive truth just as space without boundaries is not formally space. Theory, as a result, can embody truth or possibility or some mixture of the two, but it remains valid so long as the observer sees it so or if the community designates it as such. Reality, on the other hand, rather than being theoretical, is produced by the three stages I have outlined, and the distinction between the second and third stage, if there is one, depends on one's definition of style. Thus, the definition of oneself in a secular world is how we deal with the loss of innocence, awareness of the fact that what is a means for one partner to a relationship can be an end for the other, that an event for one is precedential for the other, implicating a rule by which one should abide. It is this realization that determines, and is determined by, how and whether we respond to the gap between the private and public self: the latter, which participates in the culture or sub-culture, and the former, which, when one's style is romantic, makes its own rules, as opposed to being classical, treating precedent as a substantive rather than formal rule. Justice, therefore, can be romantic or classical or mannerist.

A political act, in short, is an attempt to produce consequences, and it may or may not include taking responsibility for the choice that in theory will produce the consequence. Learning involves the taking of responsibility for what one feels ought to be done. Your paper, in other words, must be treated as a potential precedent.

Chapter 6:
A Post-Hegelian Jurisprudence: Holmes, Hand and Cardozo

PENNSYLVANIA COAL COMPANY v. MAHON ET AL.

No. 549.

SUPREME COURT OF THE UNITED STATES

260 U.S. 393; 43 S. Ct. 158; 67 L. Ed. 322; 1922 U.S. LEXIS 2381; 28 A.L.R. 1321

Argued November 14, 1922.
December 11, 1922, Decided

MR. JUSTICE HOLMES delivered the opinion of the Court.

This is a bill in equity brought by the defendants in error to prevent the Pennsylvania Coal Company from mining under their property in such way as to remove the supports and cause a subsidence of the surface and of their house. The bill sets out a deed executed by the Coal Company in 1878, under which the plaintiffs claim. The deed conveys the surface, but in express terms reserves the right to remove all the coal under the same, and the grantee takes the premises with the risk, and waives all claim for damages that may arise from mining out the coal. But the plaintiffs say that whatever may have been the Coal Company's rights, they were taken away by an Act of Pennsylvania, approved May 27, 1921, P.L. 1198, commonly known there as the Kohler Act. The Court of Common Pleas found that if not restrained the defendant would cause the damage to prevent which the bill was [***325] brought, but denied an injunction, holding that the statute if applied to this case would be unconstitutional. On appeal the Supreme Court of the State agreed that the defendant had contract and property rights protected by the Constitution of the United States, but held that the statute was a legitimate exercise of the police power and directed a decree for the plaintiffs. A writ of error was granted bringing the case to this Court.

The statute forbids the mining of anthracite coal in such way as to cause the subsidence of, among other [*413] things, any structure used as a human habitation, with certain exceptions, including among them land where the surface is owned by the owner of the underlying coal and is distant more than one hundred and fifty feet from any improved property belonging to any other person. As applied to this case the statute is admitted to destroy previously existing rights of property and contract. The question is whether the police power can be stretched so far.

Government hardly could go on if to some extent values incident to property could not be diminished without paying for every such change in the general law. As long recognized, some values are enjoyed under an implied limitation and must yield to the police power. But obviously the implied limitation must have its limits, or the contract and due process clauses are gone. One fact for consideration in determining such limits is the extent of the diminution. When it reaches a certain magnitude, in most if not in all cases there must be an exercise of eminent domain and compensation to sustain the act. So the question depends upon the particular facts. The greatest weight is given to the judgment of the legislature, but it always is open to interested parties to contend that the legislature has gone beyond its constitutional power.

This is the case of a single private house. No doubt there is a public interest even in this, as there is in every purchase and sale and in all that happens within the commonwealth. Some existing rights may be modified even in such a case. *Rideout v. Knox, 148 Mass. 368.* But usually in ordinary private affairs the public interest does not warrant much of this kind of interference. A source of damage to such a house is not a public nuisance even if similar damage is inflicted on others in different places. The damage is not common or public. *Wesson v. Washburn Iron Co., 13 Allen, 95, 103.* The extent of [*414] the public interest is shown by the statute to be limited, since the statute ordinarily does not apply to land when the surface is owned by the owner of the coal. Furthermore, it is not justified as a protection of personal safety. That could be provided for by notice. Indeed the very foundation of this bill is that the defendant gave timely notice of its intent to mine under the house. On the other hand the extent of the taking is great. It purports to abolish what is recognized in Pennsylvania as an estate in land – a very valuable estate – and what is declared by the Court below to be a contract hitherto binding the plaintiffs. If we were called upon to deal with the plaintiffs' position alone, we should think it clear that the statute does not disclose a public interest sufficient to warrant so extensive a destruction of the defendant's constitutionally protected rights.

But the case has been treated as one in which the general validity of the act should [**160] be discussed. The Attorney General of the State, the City of Scranton, and the representatives of other extensive interests were allowed to take part in the argument below and have submitted their contentions here. It seems, therefore, to be our duty to go farther in the statement of our opinion, in order that it may be known at once, and that further suits should not be brought in vain.

It is our opinion that the act cannot be sustained as an exercise of the police power, so far as it affects the mining of coal under streets or cities in places where the right to mine such coal has been reserved. As said in a Pennsylvania case, "For practical purposes, the right to coal consists in the right to mine it." *Commonwealth v. Clearview Coal Co., 256 Pa. St. 328, 331.* What makes the right to mine coal valuable is that it can be exercised with profit. To make it commercially impracticable to mine certain coal has very nearly the same effect for constitutional purposes as appropriating or destroying it. This [*415] we think that we are warranted in assuming that the statute does.

It is true that in *Plymouth Coal Co. v. Pennsylvania, 232 U.S. 531,* it was held competent for the legislature to require a pillar of coal to be left along the line of adjoining property, that, with the pillar on the other side of the line, [***326] would be a barrier sufficient for the safety of the employees of either mine in case the other should be abandoned and allowed to fill with water. But that was a requirement for the safety of employees invited into the mine, and secured an average reciprocity of advantage that has been recognized as a justification of various laws.

The rights of the public in a street purchased or laid out by eminent domain are those that it has paid for. If in any case its representatives have been so short sighted as to acquire only surface rights without the right of support, we see no more authority for supplying the latter without compensation than there was for taking the right of way in the first place and refusing to pay for it because the public wanted it very much. The protection of private property in the Fifth Amendment presupposes that it is wanted for public use, but provides that it shall not be taken for such use without compensation. A similar assumption is made in the decisions upon the *Fourteenth Amendment. Hairston v. Danville & Western Ry. Co., 208 U.S. 598, 605.* When this seemingly absolute protection is found to be qualified by the police power, the natural tendency of human nature is to extend the qualification more and more until at last private property disappears. But that cannot be accomplished in this way under the Constitution of the United States.

The general rule at least is, that while property may be regulated to a certain extent, if regulation goes too far it will be recognized as a taking. It may be doubted how far exceptional cases, like the blowing up of a house to stop a conflagration, go – and if they go beyond the general rule, [*416] whether they do not stand as much upon tradition as upon principle. *Bowditch v. Boston, 101 U.S. 16.* In general it is not plain that a man's misfortunes or necessities will justify his shifting the damages to his neighbor's shoulders. *Spade v. Lynn & Boston R.R.*

Co., 172 Mass. 488, 489. We are in danger of forgetting that a strong public desire to improve the public condition is not enough to warrant achieving the desire by a shorter cut than the constitutional way of paying for the change. As we already have said, this is a question of degree – and therefore cannot be disposed of by general propositions. But we regard this as going beyond any of the cases decided by this Court. The late decisions upon laws dealing with the congestion of Washington and New York, caused by the war, dealt with laws intended to meet a temporary emergency and providing for compensation determined to be reasonable by an impartial board. They went to the verge of the law but fell far short of the present ct. *Block v. Hirsh, 256 U.S. 135. Marcus Brown Holding Co. v. Feldman, 256 U.S. 170. Levy Leasing Co. v. Siegel, 258 U.S. 242.*

We assume, of course, that the statute was passed upon the conviction that an exigency existed that would warrant it, and we assume that an exigency exists that would warrant the exercise of eminent domain. But the question at bottom is upon whom the loss of the changes desired should fall. So far as private persons or communities have seen fit to take the risk of acquiring only surface rights, we cannot see that the fact that their risk has become a danger warrants the giving to them greater rights than they bought.

Decree reversed.

MR. JUSTICE BRANDEIS, dissenting.

The Kohler Act prohibits, under certain conditions, the mining of anthracite coal within the limits of a city in such a manner or to such an extent "as to cause the . . . [*417] subsidence of any dwelling or other structure used as a human habitation, or any factory, store, or other industrial or mercantile establishment in which human labor is employed." Coal in place is land; and the right of the owner to use his land is not absolute. He may not so use it as to create a public nuisance; and uses, once harmless, may, owing to changed conditions, seriously threaten [**161] the public welfare. Whenever they do, the legislature has power to prohibit such uses without paying compensation; and the power to prohibit extends alike to the manner, the character and the purpose of the use. Are we justified in declaring that the Legislature of Pennsylvania has, in restricting the right to mine anthracite, exercised this power so arbitrarily as to violate the Fourteenth Amendment."

Every restriction upon the use of property imposed in the exercise of the police power deprives the owner of some right theretofore enjoyed, and is, in that sense, an abridgment by the State of rights in property without making compensation. [***327] But restriction imposed to protect the public health, safety or morals from dangers threatened is not a taking. The restriction here in question is merely the prohibition of a noxious use. The property so restricted remains in the possession of its owner. The State does not appropriate it or make any use of it. The State merely prevents the owner from making a use which interferes with paramount rights of the public. Whenever the use prohibited ceases to be noxious – as it may because of further change in local or social conditions – the restriction will have to be removed and the owner will again be free to enjoy his property as heretofore.

The restriction upon the use of this property can not, of course, be lawfully imposed, unless its purpose is to protect the public. But the purpose of a restriction does not cease to be public, because incidentally some private [*418] persons may thereby receive gratuitously valuable special benefits. Thus, owners of low buildings may obtain, through statutory restrictions upon the height of neighboring structures, benefits equivalent to an easement of light and air. *Welch v. Swasey, 214 U.S. 91.* Compare *Lindsley v. Natural Carbonic Gas Co., 220 U.S. 61; Walls v. Midland Carbon Co., 254 U.S. 300.* Furthermore, a restriction, though imposed for a public purpose, will not be lawful, unless the restriction is an appropriate means to the public end. But to keep coal in place is surely an appropriate means of preventing subsidence of the surface; and ordinarily it is the only available means. Restriction upon use does not become inappropriate as a means, merely because it deprives the owner of the only use to which the property can then be profitably put. The liquor and the oleomargarine cases settled that. *Mugler v. Kansas, 123 U.S. 623, 668, 669; Powell v. Pennsylvania, 127 U.S. 678, 682.* See also *Hadacheck v. Los Angeles, 239 U.S. 394; Pierce Oil Corporation v. City of Hope, 248 U.S. 498.* Nor is a restriction imposed through exercise of the police power inappropriate as a means, merely because the same end might be effected through exercise of the power of eminent domain, or otherwise at public expense. Every restriction upon the height of buildings might be secured through acquiring by eminent domain the right of each owner to build above the limiting height; but it is settled that the State need not resort to that power.

Compare *Laurel Hill Cemetery v. San Francisco*, 216 U.S. 358; *Missouri Pacific Ry. Co. v. Omaha*, 235 U.S. 121. If by mining anthracite coal the owner would necessarily unloose poisonous gasses, I suppose no one would doubt the power of the State to prevent the mining, without buying his coal fields. And why may not the State, likewise, without paying compensation, prohibit one from digging so deep or excavating so near the surface, as to expose the community to [*419] like dangers? In the latter case, as in the former, carrying on the business would be a public nuisance.

It is said that one fact for consideration in determining whether the limits of the police power have been exceeded is the extent of the resulting diminution in value; and that here the restriction destroys existing rights of property and contract. But values are relative. If we are to consider the value of the coal kept in place by the restriction, we should compare it with the value of all other parts of the land. That is, with the value not of the coal alone, but with the value of the whole property. The rights of an owner as against the public are not increased by dividing the interests in his property into surface and subsoil. The sum of the rights in the parts can not be greater than the rights in the whole. The estate of an owner in land is grandiloquently described as extending ab orco usque ad coelum. But I suppose no one would contend that by selling his interest above one hundred feet from the surface he could prevent the State from limiting, by the police power, the height of structures in a city. And why should a sale of underground rights bar the State's power? For aught that appears the value of the coal kept in place by the restriction may be negligible as compared with the value of the whole property, or even as compared with that part of it which is represented by the coal remaining in place and which may be extracted despite the statute. Ordinarily a police regulation, general in operation, will not be held void as to a particular property, although proof is offered that owing to conditions peculiar to it the restriction could not reasonably be applied. See *Powell v. Pennsylvania,* [***328] *127 U.S. 678, 681, 684; Murphy v. California, 225 U.S. 623, 629.* But even if the particular [**162] facts are to govern, the statute should, in my opinion, be upheld in this case. For the defendant has failed to adduce any evidence from which [*420] it appears that to restrict its mining operations was an unreasonable exercise of the police power. Compare *Reinman v. Little Rock, 237 U.S. 171, 177, 180; Pierce Oil Corporation v. City of Hope, 248 U.S. 498, 500.* Where the surface and the coal belong to the same person, self-interest would ordinarily prevent mining to such an extent as to cause a subsidence. It was, doubtless, for this reason that the legislature, estimating the degrees of danger, deemed statutory restriction unnecessary for the public safety under such conditions.

It is said that this is a case of a single dwelling house; that the restriction upon mining abolishes a valuable estate hitherto secured by a contract with the plaintiffs; and that the restriction upon mining cannot be justified as a protection of personal safety, since that could be provided for by notice. The propriety of deferring a good deal to tribunals on the spot has been repeatedly recognized. *Welch v. Swasey, 214 U.S. 91, 106; Laurel Hill Cemetery v. San Francisco, 216 U.S. 358, 365; Patsone v. Pennsylvania, 232 U.S. 138, 144.* May we say that notice would afford adequate protection of the public safety where the legislature and the highest court of the State, which greater knowledge of local conditions, have declared, in effect, that it would not? If public safety is imperiled, surely neither grant, nor contract, can prevail against the exercise of the police power. *Fertilizing Co. v. Hyde Park, 97 U.S. 659; Atlantic Coast Line R.R. Co. v. Goldsboro, 232 U.S. 548; Union Dry Goods Co. v. Georgia Public Service Corporation, 248 U.S. 372; St. Louis Poster Advertising Co. v. St. Louis, 249 U.S. 269.* The rule that the State's power to take appropriate measures to guard the safety of all who may be within its jurisdiction may not be bargained away was applied to compel carriers to establish grade crossings at their own expense, despite contracts to the contrary; *Chicago, Burlington & Quincy R.R. Co. v. Nebraska, 170 U.S. 57;* [*421] and, likewise, to supersede, by an employers' liability act, the provision of a charter exempting a railroad from liability for death of employees, since the civil liability was deemed a matter of public concern, and not a mere private right. *Texas & New Orleans R.R. Co. v. Miller, 221 U.S. 408.* Compare *Boyd v. Alabama, 94 U.S. 645; Stone v. Mississippi, 101 U.S. 814; Butchers' Union Co. v. Crescent City Co., 111 U.S. 746; Douglas v. Kentucky, 168 U.S. 488; Pennsylvania Hospital v. Philadelphia, 245 U.S. 20, 23.* Nor can existing contracts between private individuals preclude exercise of the police power. "One whose rights, such as they are, are subject to state restriction, cannot remove them from the power of the State by making a contract about them." *Hudson County Water Co. v. McCarter, 209 U.S. 349, 357; Knoxville Water Co. v. Knoxville, 189 U.S. 434, 438; Rast v. Van Deman & Lewis*

Co., 240 U.S. 342. The fact that this suit is brought by a private person is, of course, immaterial to protect the community through invoking the aid, as litigant, of interested private citizens is not a novelty in our law. That it may be done in Pennsylvania was decided by its Supreme Court in this case. And it is for a State to say how its public policy shall be enforced.

This case involves only mining which causes subsidence of a dwelling house. But the Kohler Act contains provisions in addition to that quoted above; and as to these, also, an opinion is expressed. These provisions deal with mining under cities to such an extent as to cause subsidence of --

(a) Any public building or any structure customarily used by the public as a place of resort, assemblage, or amusement, including, but not being limited to, [***329] churches, schools, hospitals, theatres, hotels, and railroad stations.

(b) Any street, road, bridge, or other public passageway, dedicated to public use or habitually used by the public.

[*422] (c) Any track, roadbed, right of way, pipe, conduit, wire, or other facility, used in the service of the public by any municipal corporation or public service company as defined by the Public Service Company Law.

A prohibition of mining which causes subsidence of such structures and facilities is obviously enacted for a public purpose; and it seems, likewise, clear that mere notice of intention to mine would not in this connection secure the public safety. Yet it is said that these provisions of the act cannot be sustained as an exercise of the police power where the right to mine such coal has been reserved. The conclusion seems to rest upon the assumption that in order to justify such exercise of the police power there must be "an average reciprocity of advantage" as between the owner of the property restricted and the rest of the community; and that here such reciprocity is absent. Reciprocity [**163] of advantage is an important consideration, and may even be an essential, where the State's power is exercised for the purpose of conferring benefits upon the property of a neighborhood, as in drainage projects, *Wurts v. Hoagland, 114 U.S. 606; Fallbrook Irrigation District v. Bradley, 164 U.S. 112;* or upon adjoining owners, as by party wall provisions, Jackman v. Rosenbaum Co., ante, 22. But where the police power is exercised, not to confer benefits upon property owners, but to protect the public from detriment and danger, there is, in my opinion, no room for considering reciprocity of advantage. There was no reciprocal advantage to the owner prohibited from using his oil tanks in *248 U.S. 498*; his brickyard, in *239 U.S. 394*; his livery stable, in *237 U.S. 171*; his billiard hall, in *225 U.S. 623*; his oleomargarine factory, in *127 U.S. 678*; his brewery, in *123 U.S. 623*; unless it be the advantage of living and doing business in a civilized community. That reciprocal advantage is given by the act to the coal operators.

Given *Kelo v. New London*, is *Mahon* a valid precedent?

Scientific formulas, which Holmes accepted as authoritative, function as rational habits. This perspective permits one to treat cultural choices – the extent to which property is private rather than social for example – as a social science datum, thus transforming an emotional judicial choice into an objective truth, a certainty denied to Hand. Precedent, however, is central to the rule of common law, and Hand's treatment of it can accurately be classified as classical, postulating Utopia in the present.

Cardozo's opinions made history by becoming precedents, but they in effect disregarded precedent because his opinions stood only for themselves, neither governed by the past nor defining the boundaries that limited their application. He was enabled to do this because his opinions, like all romantic creations, embodied a personal metaphor: that a strongly held emotional truth freezes time, thus eliminating the need for history.

Neither Holmes nor Hand is a romantic. Their approaches to precedent are strikingly different, however, despite the fact that Hand greatly admired Holmes. For Hand, precedent is the Platonic Form of the Good, whereas Holmes, being a cynic, does not distinguish good from evil except in operational terms.

Do you agree? If not, why not? If so, is Utopia cynical, realistic as well as aspirational, just as mannerism is acknowledgement of substantive limitations as well as technical possibilities? As to *Mahon*, is Brandeis approaching the question of the right at issue as

Niebuhr would whereas Holmes' approach parallels that taken by Tillich to the question of the nature of the Divinity?

The Mystery of Law

Whether the judge is responsible for her or his perspective, whether a personal culture is mannerist, is itself a metaphorical question, an attempt to treat style as objective truth. Do you agree? If not, why not? If so, do you agree that precedent is the product of style? If not, why not? If so, is precedent private or public?

Q. I assume that last question is unanswerable. If so, why do you ask?

A. To make clear the central role of mystery in a workable jurisprudence.

Q. What's the mystery? Privacy is immunity from legal regulation, liberty as opposed to freedom. And public is social, the basis for culture.

A. That may be true in a republic where either party or government defines the boundary between public and private, but you want a constitutional republic.

Q. I just want what we have in the United States, a democracy in which everyone has the right to be free, to live as an aristocrat.

A. You mean to have what they feel entitled to, the sort of fascist republic Huey Long created in Louisiana.

Q. I never denied that populists could do evil. Why do you think Long is relevant? Why isn't what matters that Franklin Roosevelt saw the danger he represented?

A. I assume you aren't implying that Roosevelt had so much influence that the disgruntled citizen who assassinated Long was an instrumental tool rather than a hero making a statement about life and liberty. You seem to forget that de Tocqueville had real concerns about what you designate populism, and what I regard as the public manifestation of democratic power.

Q. Surely you're not arguing that populism is always bad?

A. My philosophy says that progressivism is different from populism because it wins, and is therefore treated as inevitable (even if not valuable) by historians.

Q. So you agree there's a distinction between fact and value?

A. Yes. It's the distinction between the legal opinion and the precedent.

Q. That may be true if law is applied politics, but we're arguing about de Tocqueville, and when he wrote your definition of law was not yet operational.

A. In artistic terms, I agree that law in the Jacksonian era was perceived as classical without romantic elements, doing what history required rather than engaging in revolution, but remember that France in the Jacksonian era meant Napoleon as well as revolution, and that Jackson, like Napoleon, was a post-revolutionary general who regarded Great Britain as the enemy, power as something necessary to defend against Great Britain, and revolution as historical truth rather than future necessity.

Q. So your jurisprudence is post-Hegelian because Hegel's Prussia – his synthesis – was part of the alliance that defeated Napoleon, and did so with an army that was becoming national rather than feudal. But what of the fact that it was Spartan rather than Athenian, a single tribe rather than the cosmopolitan society in which we live? Thus, I'll grant that influence and power, like private and public, are continuous spectra rather than choices, that freedom is the ability to make choices, and that culture defines the choices we make, just as I'll grant that economics – the "market" – is simply the present masquerading as a competitive process; but one must act sometimes, and a good philosophy presumably informs us about the decisions underlying our actions.

A. Those decisions are what my philosophy designates emotional, and neutrality is the word we use to signal that emotion has given way to rationality. Both philosophy and jurisprudence are instrumental tools, attempts to persuade about the validity of a given view of reality, but the ultimate mystery is when a tool becomes substantive, a value rather than a fact, and Hegel is the last philosopher to believe in a systematic answer to that question.

My philosophy treats facts as questions of epistemology and values as questions of ethics. The former are matters of science, the use of mathematics to transform the symbols known as words into functional signs, a process that produces the formulas in accordance with which rational action can take place. Ethics is a matter of pain, something which indicates the need for change, and pleasure, a purely personal concept whose public manifestation is the absence of pain. The political judgment, therefore, is whether a situation is painful, and the extent of other humans' agreement with that judgment, whether, in short, it is time for a revolution or war.

Q. I'll grant all that, because I accept that you have simply articulated the theoretical basis for what you term inertia and momentum, but is the proper timing for a revolution or war – the attempt to produce a change – a matter of art or science?

A. You're once again confusing instrumental and substantive. Perhaps the problem is that your republic is capitalist, in which power is financial as well as political. Thus, art is the ultimate moral determinant in that it creates symbols by describing reality as it was or can be and thus creates goals that are liberal or conservative, romantic or classical. It is those goals that power emotional decisions, political actions which lead to outcomes history will characterize as progressive or populist, good or evil or unsuccessful. Just because you can buy art, however, does not mean that you understand its value except in monetary terms, what it will fetch in the market today. To understand value in non-monetary terms, you must master the difference between fact and value, between a legal opinion and a precedent.

Q. All right. How does one master that mystery?

A. By accepting that science – the contemporary orthodoxy – is no different from art insofar as instrumentality can become substance and possibility truth. Thus, mathematics is where art and science overlap; and ethics and epistemology overlap because where we want to go – to measure the degree of change needed or to locate position, the status quo – determines how we get there from here. A mathematical sign is technical because it is clear, a certain direction, but if we apply it we are engaging in theory, basing present behavior on a relationship, an equivalence, that occurred in the past. We are, in short, ignoring the dimension of time. When a sign fails adequately to fulfill its function, it is because of context, possibly a change in the environment which has changed one of the entities connected by an equal sign; and the general formulation of this epistemological problem is that a successful sign, one that is currently being applied, is in fact functioning as a symbol, as something which bridges the gap that the present constitutes between the past and the future.

Precedent is a legal opinion functioning as a political tool because in theory it has not changed. Analogously, quantum is a fixed unit which provides the theoretical basis for measuring the force needed to move mass. Motion, the historical progression that embodies change, is produced by force and accounted for in terms of inertia and momentum. The new entity or entities produced by change are therefore simultaneously epistemologically substantive – something produced by the quantum – and theoretically instrumental, something whose function is to prove that the theory works, that the formula is valid. Whether the mathematical formula is itself an artificial imposition or an accurate approximation of reality is the mystery, and when the application is successful, it hints at the possibility of order produced by a Higher Power.

The legal order is an analogous mystery. The opinion articulates how the context known as culture manifests itself in a particular situation. The theoretical possibility that the opinion will become a precedent is what commands obedience because, if one has faith, spiritual and material power are not necessarily contradictory and are therefore separated only by law without equity, only because human institutions compete. The ethical question, therefore, is the private question of the possibility of humility, whether the pride needed to compete will be balanced by the love needed to cooperate. My question is whether the socioeconomic environment is such that fraternity has ceased to be an operational political symbol because proper behavior has become synonymous with liberty. If so, politics will be narrowed to pursuing the goals of eliminating waste and corruption rather than pursuing the aspiration of Hegelian freedom, liberty as responsibility, a behavioral burden which enables one to strive, not for what one wants or what one believes will benefit society, but for the complexity of a truth that is valid both ethically and epistemologically, the ambiguity of attempting to do the right thing, a goal that is simultaneously successful and spiritual.

Q. What advantage is gained by following your political philosophy, replacing individual rights with acceptance of a vision of life as process? Even Aristotle never accepted your view that the substance of the Platonic Form could be reduced to humility, to the social attempt to make individuals responsible.

A. My philosophy makes fraternity a theoretical possibility by making equality recognition of the uncertainty each of us constitutes for ourselves, each other, and society, the changing sense of self that justifies equity in limiting the power of law.

Q. But the first Federal Rule of Civil Procedure merged law and equity.

A. And that is when American law lost its sacred character, when it became logical to treat it as solely instrumental, as the manifestation of a social science rather than the art of applied politics.

Q. Why do you say sacred? The people who drafted the Constitution that makes American law powerful may have been Deists, but their feelings about religion were at best contradictory.

A. The short answer is that a good judge is spiritual despite having to be a cynic. The argument is that the Higher Power, like all social truth, is metaphoric, a symbol as much as a sign, and therefore most persuasive when it is mathematical, when the social need for order can be felt to be rational rather than emotional. Mathematical truth is an abstract mystery; law, when you are subject to it, is concrete power.

Q. But are good judges possible?

A. Is the right result?

Q. Even if I accept all this uncertainty, must I accept your view? What, for example, is culture in an operational context?

A. Socially, it is the exercise of discretion justified as expertise; personally, it is the justification for deferring gratification. In America, however, the overriding social fact is diversity. Thus, in a revolution, law does not function as a symbol of unity; and when, as in RICO, law is directed against social enemies, it is a weapon, a means of coercion. In other contexts, however, at least in America, law *is* the culture.

Q. And exactly how do the personal metaphors that create culture overlap?

A. By defining roles whose performance is cultural behavior, providing the basis for political judgments. In a nation, as opposed to a tribe or an empire, such judgments are subject to rational scrutiny in an ongoing attempt to reconcile the secular, liberal, aspirations of Rousseau with the conservative longings of Hobbes. Niebuhr and

Tillich proposed alternative versions of the faith that makes such a reconciliation possible, and Tillich's version is available to those liberals and conservatives who do not define themselves as potential sinners.

A. Suppose I accept all of this. The question remains whether or not we can have good law even without good judges.

A. Why isn't the result in the O.J. Simpson trial the answer, the precedent that illustrates what happens when a judge loses control of the trial?

Q. Because it's only one instance rather than a precedent.

A. I am humbly certain you may be right. Are you certain that I am entitled to the same humility on your part?

www.ingramcontent.com/pod-product-compliance
Ingram Content Group UK Ltd.
Pitfield, Milton Keynes, MK11 3LW, UK
UKHW051250180426
11947UKWH00020B/1642